CW00405862

APLEY HALL

The Golden Years
of a Sporting Estate

APLEY HALL

The Golden Years of a Sporting Estate

Norman Sharpe

With a Foreword by Edward Sharpe

MERLIN UNWIN BOOKS

First published in Great Britain by Merlin Unwin Books, 2009

Text © The Estate of Norman Sharpe, 2009

All rights reserved, including the right to reproduce this book or portions thereof in any form or by any means, electronic or mechanical, including photocopying, recording, or by an information storage and retrieval system, without permission from the publisher. All enquiries should be addressed to:

Merlin Unwin Books Ltd
Palmers House
7 Corve Street
Ludlow, Shropshire SY8 1DB
U.K.

www.merlinunwin.co.uk
email: books@merlinunwin.co.uk

The author asserts his moral right to be identified as the author of this work.
A CIP catalogue record for this book is available from the British Library.

ISBN 978-1-906122-16-4

Designed and set in Bembo by Merlin Unwin
Printed and bound in the UK by TJ International Ltd, Padstow

CONTENTS

TO THE COUNTRYSIDE

*May God bless the efforts of all who strive to
maintain and improve it.*

I gave a copy to my
shoot Commander a great
friend Nick Mason, in late
2009
for christmas

APLEY HALL
and its surrounding estate

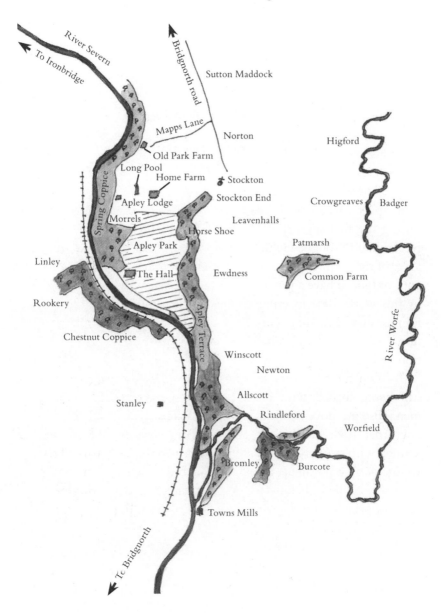

FOREWORD

Norman Sharpe grew up on a sporting estate in the glorious county of Shropshire. His father had taken the position of Head Gamekeeper on the estate in 1902 and Norman succeeded him in 1928. In these recollections he dwells not only on the sheer beauty of the place, but also the richness of its wildlife, diversity of its sport, and of course the folk who lived and worked there during the first seventy years of the twentieth century. All are recalled and brought vividly back to life. If, like him, you are a lover of the countryside, share his fascination for its wild inhabitants, or indeed have a yen for social history, you will be captivated by this work. Bear in mind these were years of extreme change for man and beast alike. Furthermore it was a passage of time split into three distinct and completely disparate phases by the disruption and upheaval of two world wars.

During the years leading up to 1914, cartridges were still being loaded with black powder, the Ironbridge coracle men, absolute doyens of the poaching fraternity, still plied their nocturnal trade, curleycoat and flatcoat retrievers shared the kennels with spaniels, the cart horse still ruled the land, partridges were shot by walking up, aeroplanes had only just taken wing, the cane was applied liberally to young offenders and hunting held pride of place on the sporting agenda. Finally, and quoting from his text, 'Though wages were still low, and the hours worked far too long, there was a contentment and certainty in the way of life for all sections of the community which has never been replaced.'

1

Then came the Great War!

1915 saw Norman journey north to the land of his forebears to enlist in the Argyll and Sutherland Highlanders. After two and a half years in the mud and blood of the trenches his long run of luck finally appeared to have run out when he was severely wounded. Another great stroke of good fortune still awaited, though, for he found himself in the care of an Irish nurse, a Sister Read, but for whose quite inspirational skill he would most assuredly have died. But that is another story.

At his final medical board he was informed in no uncertain terms that physical work could never be an option for him. He would have to seek sedentary employment! How little they could have realised the character of the man before them. Thought of a boring routine within the confines of four walls was anathema to that free spirit. Possessed of immense determination he was also blessed with a resilient physique and in his own words, 'really punished himself until his legs finally did what he wished of them.' At long last, in 1921, he threw aside his second stick and began work as a gamekeeper under his father.

1924 had witnessed the death of the old squire and ownership of the estate pass to his son. There followed a dramatic increase in the range and number of guests staying at Apley Hall. They arrived in many guises: diplomats, politicians, show business celebrities, literary folk, many of the leading titles in the land, even royalty on occasion. Sport was to become a key element in their entertainment and it was decided to intensify every aspect of it across the estate. Responsibility for putting all this into practice fell to the author of this work.

Partridge driving was introduced, the Euston system was employed and two teams of beaters operated on shooting days. Nobel smokeless had replaced black powder and pairs of guns and loaders became the norm. In the kennels, flats and curlies surrendered pride of place to the Labrador retriever and on the rearing field mincer, chopper and copper, those stalwarts of yesteryear gave way to complete diets supplied in hessian sacks and delivered by lorries.

On the farms a few tractors appeared but for the most part Dobbin remained the main source of power. Brushing hook and hand hoe, muck fork and pykel remained essential tools to be powered only by muscle and sweat. For the first time in living memory there was fishing for salmon on the estate waters of the Severn and a river keeper was employed in order to improve trout fishing on the river Worfe. Wildlife continued to flourish in as great a variety and profusion as ever before. Large bags of pheasants and partridges were being recorded. Norman Sharpe had established himself as a regular contributor to the sporting press of the day including a couple of chapters in the Keepers' volume of the Lonsdale Library. There was an invitation to broadcast on the BBC's Overseas network. That never happened for there came another war!

After 1945 a very different scene prevailed. Gone now the flamboyance and euphoria of the Thirties. Keepering staff reduced, the survival of shooting, indeed of the estates themselves was far from certain. Not until the early Fifties were pheasants reared again on a greatly reduced scale. On the land we were witnessing the greatest upheaval since the Enclosure Acts. Hedges planted then were now being torn out as cart horse and manual worker were finally swept away by tractor and technology. The whole scene was one of accelerating and unrelenting change. Change for the better in so many respects. Change for the worse in others, for his final passages quite graphically describe the poisoning of a great river and the countryside through which it flows.

Fifties saw salmon catches peak before beginning to fall rapidly away. Sixties witnessed the near total demise of his favourite bird, the grey partridge. Alas not only the salmon and partridge, where accurate records preclude all argument, but a whole host of other less obvious species. Mammals, birds, insects, reptiles; their demise could not be so accurately plotted. Many species were completely decimated and so far as the estate was concerned, actually ceased to exist. This work vividly conveys the sheer scale of the disaster which at the time appeared to pass largely unnoticed.

Changes in farming practice had certainly not helped but even in those early days Norman was in no doubt regarding the identity of the prime culprits, i.e. farm chemicals, though at the time of course their innocence was being furiously protested by the powerful commercial interests responsible for their development and distribution.

So run the recollections of seventy years. Invariably they are portrayed with clarity, for the most part with a considerable degree of humour, finally with great sadness by an author gifted with quite exceptional powers of observation and blessed with an intense love of that glorious tract of Shropshire over which he and his father before him were privileged to serve as custodians for sixty-six unforgettable years.

Edward Sharpe
Ingleby, Lincoln
2009

1

THE DOG GLEN

It was many, many years ago when I received that letter from home. It was in fact the bitter winter of 1916; the place, those torn shattered trenches, or rather ditches of mud where fighting had been relentlessly savage and prolonged. Even today the earthy stale aroma of decaying bags reawakens memories of the battle-front of the Somme. There was not a lot in the letter: the usual account of local happenings, news of other boys, telling of woundings, maybe a pal's death, perhaps even a cutting from the local paper recording same under the heading 'Killed in Action'.

Recorded at the very end of my letter was 'Poor old Glen passed peacefully away. As you know he has been poorly for some time. Yesterday he came into the house and seemed much livelier and when your father got up this morning he thought at first that he was better. His head was leaning on his paws and he appeared to be looking out, but had died in his sleep. How quickly moments of gladness can turn to moments of sadness! Rarely have I shed tears in my adult life; that was one occasion. Memories of the dear old boy have never faded and remain fresh in my mind to this day although so many other things seemingly of greater importance are long since forgotten'.

But back to the beginning of the story, which takes us away to a drizzly, dripping night in November when every twig and blade of grass was beaded with droplets of moisture. Two small boys, their faces pressed against a steaming window trying to pierce the murk, searching eagerly for a glimpse of trap lights. Hurried dashes to the outside door to listen for the clop clop of pony hooves. At long last hoof beats and a rattle of wheels; soon and surprisingly close, lights dimpling out of the mist to be followed by a 'Whoa Boy'. By this time we were out in the yard and our father reached down a hamper which was carried carefully into the house. Eager anticipation as we waited for him to come in but first there was the pony's welfare to attend to.

At long last the hamper was opened. There sitting in it after his long journey from the north of Scotland was Glen, so named already by our uncle who had given him to us boys. Just three months old he was a Springer spaniel of most excellent pedigree. In fact his mother had won the first Spaniel Trial ever held.

When one is very young, first impressions can be both vivid and extremely enduring. For I still recall with clarity a picture that has never dimmed of the puppy we now so proudly owned, can still capture the intelligence in his face and the appeal from those deep honest eyes. Moreover there was the quiet friendly dignity, an early pointer to what his character would become. His colouring was a rich liver and white, the latter more flecked than pure and he had a small tan patch above each eye.

Throughout his puppy days Glen had sleeping quarters in the harness room. Across the yard was a beautiful range of kennels which in those days were populated by curlycoats, flatcoats and spaniels. These were taken out in turn by my father and of course that meant leaving Glen in the harness room. Not for long though! By jumping onto a table he managed to knock open the window latch. When that was secured with wire he turned his attention to the door. A good leap was needed to reach the latch but even so it was quickly opened. To counter this the latch slot was plugged with a wooden wedge. There was however a tall corn bin conveniently sited to one side of the door. A leap onto this gave the lad a base from which he could balance on a cross support and so reach the latch handle. By banging long enough on that with a paw he was able to loosen the wedge and be free. The patience and determination required to achieve this was truly amazing. Next he was put into one of the range of kennels. Only one dog, a wise old curlie answering to the name of Shot, had ever succeeded in freeing itself. Hardly surprising as the latches were shoulder-height and secured by the slot in a sliding horizontal bar dropping over a vertical catch. Apart from the upward leap opening them entailed both a vertical and horizontal push. Many a dog managed the leap and sideways push; only Shot had ever mastered the double movement. Within a few minutes Glen had solved the problem and was out!

After this the only time an effort was made to fasten him up were the occasions he was not taken out on shooting days. Several times he escaped after Father had left and by taking the short cut through the wood was able to meet them in the courtyard of the Hall which was always the first stop. This was a bad mistake on his part as he was frustrated either by being taken home by the boy or spending the day in a stable loose box which defied even his Houdini talents. Later efforts were, from his point of view, altogether more satisfactory. He allowed the trap an extra mile or two start before catching up with it and so made sure of his day's pleasure.

A kennel on the drying green, where the washing was hung out, finally became Glen's permanent headquarters. When first attached to the chain he slipped his collar. It was tightened and he slipped it again. A further adjustment which must have been uncomfortable to say the very least appeared to have finally beaten the lad. Soon however there were urgent enquiries as to who had let Glen off the chain. My brother and I were the chief suspects. Still, relief usually comes to the innocent, for Glen got free again when our involvement was out of the question.

It was some time before he was actually seen freeing himself. The clip in use was a strong one and required really firm pressure to open it. This was further strengthened but without success. One day a friend of the family was visiting us and Father was telling him about it. He inspected the chain and clip and after some hesitation said he just could not believe it. It was absolutely impossible! So a demonstration was arranged. Whilst our visitor and my father watched from an upstairs window, brother Ted, complete with gun and game bag, left in full view of the dog.

Exactly how this escape was achieved we never really knew. All I can do is try and describe the antics. First he backed away until the chain was taut. Then – a sudden fling round of his head, a lightning half-twist and snatch – and the lad was off! So ended any attempt to tie or fasten him up. One is almost loath to record this chain episode for it is difficult to believe, but it is true nevertheless and numerous people were given the opportunity to witness it.

In those days a large flock of hens was kept and if the yard gate was left open they came through onto the drying green. Glen was encouraged to see them off and this he did most cheerfully with the exception of one particular hen which made her nest in his box. He even left his kennel for her to go in and lay; then collected the egg and delivered it into the house intact! How this all came about and exactly why this particular hen was favoured is anyone's guess. I suspect the first occasion must have occurred when he was absent.

In the Spring, newly-hatched coops of pheasant chicks were frequently put out on the drying green. Glen took a great interest in these. We often scattered food over his body and he laid there quite contentedly whilst they scrambled over him and ate it.

Two iron wicket gates opened into the garden. With push-down fasteners some thirty inches from ground level they were easily opened by the dog. Another tallish wooden gate leading into the wood he had to jump. When snow covered the ground his beat was easily followed. A well trodden track starting from his kennel, a jump over an iron fence into the yard and across to the hen houses, then into the wood via the garden, back along a path beneath a cliff of sandstone and so round to his kennel again. Lying in bed at night one could hear the snap of the iron wickets as they closed and knew that Glen was on his nightly patrol. Many a sitting hen which had stolen her nest was saved from the fox by his vigilance. Only twice during that period can I recall Charlie having any success. On one occasion the hen minus her tail feathers; another one so badly injured she had to be destroyed.

Foxes were numerous and Glen's constant worry. Sometimes a litter of cubs was dug out and temporarily housed in the Slaughter House. Throughout the night he rarely left that door and no rest for him at those times! Sometimes, when sitting on the garden seat at the north end of the house my father used to say, 'Shhhh... is that a fox, Glen?' Immediately he was all attention, ears straining, nose to the wood. Finally, when no whiff of fox had reached him, he flopped down again and scrubbed his back along the box edging; several yards opposite that seat never did flourish. At other times, and completely on his own accord, he had been known to stiffen with nose twitching, then dash down the path and into the wood with a flying leap over the gate; sometimes away for an appreciable time and on returning was well puffed!

After being taken to the woods at about six weeks of age, young pheasants were night watched until they were safely at roost. An old fox was giving a lot of trouble at Morrells. Charlie Wall was the watchman and on this particular night Father and one or two others were waiting in the hope of getting a shot at the culprit. In the dim light Reynard was seen entering a break of bracken but with no chance of a shot.

Glen was given the word to go and was heard giving the odd yelp near the Hall. Time elapsed and he did not return so the little party went in search of him. Finally they found him in the courtyard of the Hall, that veritable bastion of hunting, proudly guarding his dead fox. There was doubtless a hustle to remove the trophy!

Training dogs to perform tricks is not something I am enamoured with for they can become a bit of a nuisance at times. For all that it must be confessed we boys did have great fun teaching Glen. Probably his star turn was to beg and when told to sing he used to beat the air with his fore paws whilst emitting as weird a chant as you ever heard. He loved to be dressed up. We never succeeded in getting him to smoke his pipe, but he could be persuaded to hold one which had been smoked. He was only too pleased to die for you at any time and came to life with an expectant spring for the reward – being a firm believer in pay for a job well done!

Entering into all our games and activities Glen became so much a part of our lives. A most useful fielder he soon learned the difference between a hard cricket ball and a soft tennis ball; the one he picked up and carried only when it had lost its speed, the other he snapped up and caught like lightning.

As a water dog he was great and I must record one incident which, for me, provided conclusive proof that dogs do think and are not governed entirely by associations and instinct. It was the end of the shooting season and on a cocking day a bird shot from a spinney abutting onto the Severn collapsed on the opposite bank. Glen swam across but a strong volume of water swept him a long way downstream. Shaking himself he quickly made back and picking up the line where the bird had fallen took it up over the railway line and into the adjoining wood.

After a short time he returned to the river bank and placing the bird on the ground retained it with a paw. As they watched he finally picked his bird up and trotted away upstream until out of sight. Somebody saw him crossing the suspension bridge a

Glen was always fondly remembered by Norman and his brother

good half mile up river and he finally delivered the pheasant to my father and waiting group of men. At the time the river was swollen from recent rains and his brain had convinced him that the current would have been too strong for him to swim back with the bird. He had worked out that the only way to complete his retrieve was over the bridge.

Another great retrieve comes to mind. A cock pheasant which was shot near the house could not be found. Glen was not with the party so my father sent someone for him. He quickly picked the line up and disappeared from view. As it was the end of the day it was decided to wait no longer but to go home. Half an hour later we had all sat down to tea when Glen swaggered triumphantly in with a strong runner, hardly a feather displaced. He was well and truly mucked up and bedraggled and, as you may guess, the moment he was relieved of the bird, gave himself an almighty shake! Being somewhat house-proud I am afraid my mother did not appreciate his achievement to the full.

One of Glen's dislikes, a very big one, was shown by his annoyance when the hunt visited us. This stemmed from an incident one morning when a wet miserable little dog was waiting by the back door. His condition was fully explained when we noticed his kennel held a new occupant; a foxhound which had lost itself during the previous day's hunting had managed to get in and take possession. He must have slipped in when Glen was on patrol and it was an easy matter to hold the fort with its narrow entrance. After that Glen was friendly to all breeds except foxhounds!

In the days of which I write, dog medicines were limited. Go into a pet shop today and the array might lead you to think you are at the chemist's. Bob Martin's condition powders and Shirley's canker powder held the fort for years. Dogs were frequently dosed, Castor Oil and Buckthorn being the great standby. One glimpse of that bottle and the lad was missing. Of course the poor blighter always got his quota in the end. This revives memories of the vile concoctions we youngsters were made to swallow, Dr. Gregory's powder, liquorice powder and castor oil. Glory be 'Zenna Tea' was before my time but the adults told harrowing tales of it. Dear old Glen, our sympathies were with you. We had much in common!

◇◇◇◇◇◇◇◇◇

2

FISH ALIVO!

Old people often say they remember their early childhood quite clearly. That is not true in my own case. For instance I cannot even recall what our home in Essex looked like, though I do remember the slow blue flame from a fringed mantle-piece cover I had put a match to; also my father's hustle in putting it out!

His name escapes me, but the youth who did all the odd jobs demonstrated a trick, pretending to slap the palm of his hand down on to a needle sticking from the bench we were sitting on. My attempt drove it clean through my hand and I can still see the point sticking through the skin. Doubtless I yelled and Father arrived on the scene. Whilst he was looking for a pair of pliers the youth attempted to draw it with his teeth, but only succeeded in breaking it off, which entailed a visit to the doctor.

One memory stands out more vividly than any other. We were taken fishing. Those fish we caught fascinated me for to my young eyes they were lovely large creatures with beautiful colours. My guess today is that they were gudgeon! From that first outing may well have sprung a lifetime's dedication to angling

So we leave Essex with the fading picture of a paddock colourful with wild flowers which grew there in profusion and beyond it a large wood.

Memories of early days at Apley are altogether more vivid and so many events are recalled with a clarity which is remarkable. Of course my brother and I were growing up, our interests widening with each passing day. Looking back how full and varied a life we led.

Our lives quickly developed into a kind of double existence; the school door the frontier. For some reason the school master of the day just never saw eye to eye with me. He was a great believer in the cane and at one period of my school life few days went by without me being well and truly tickled up. For a few whom he deemed the worst offenders he kept a special cane. Needless to say I was one of that select company! If whacking really is a stimulant to growth I surely should have been an outsize specimen!

Today it hardly seems believable but I never complained to my parents. In fact the schoolmaster was a frequent visitor at our house sharing as he did a common interest in beekeeping with my father. On going to bed I was always made to kiss him goodnight and believe me that hurt me more than any caning ever did!

Do not imagine though that he had things all his own way. Even now I can see him legging it up and down between three or four long rows of kidney beans, my brother and I having done a little preparatory work on his bee veil before he and Father approached the hives.

At playtime the games played were seasonal and they came round as regularly as the clock. Sunday-Monday was a ball game played off a wall and was very popular. Like so many of our games, Tops were played on the King's highway for it was an event to see a car go through and there was always a race to look at it. In dry weather they created a choking cloud of dust and road verges and hedges were smothered in it.

Marbles were a great standby and there were bitter battles when the conker season came round, but the joy of all was Bung-The-Barrel. Any number could play, but two teams of six was ideal. One boy placed his back to a wall, the next wedged his head into the first one's stomach and the remainder bent with heads to backsides. With flying jumps the opposing team attempted to break the bridge formed by the first team. If all landed without touching the ground and were held up long enough for a now-forgotten ditty to be gasped out – the first team were the winners. Rough but great fun!

Paper chases were another prime favourite and greatly enjoyed. Hockey played in the boys' playground was also a winner. On the other side of the wall was the Police Station and how lucky we have been with our policemen. Believe me the Bobby was greatly respected and if he drew his cane across some young offender's backside the punishment was summary and just and, as a deterrent, very effective!

Cricket was taken extremely seriously at school. At that time this was true of most of the local village schools and as a result the senior game benefited greatly. My first match, when I would have been about twelve, was against Worfield school some six miles distant. We journeyed there by horse and traps belonging to the agent, the clerk of the works and the publican. I made the top score of over fifty and took several wickets; the occasion was complete as we won and were all given real cricketing caps, dark blue with gold piping. That was a day to remember!

During our boyhood, egg collecting was all the rage with adults and youngsters alike. Over the years we built up a really good collection and there were very few local species it did not include. Father always instilled into us that we should never take more than one from each clutch. You may rest assured we rigidly adhered to that edict! Our locality was perfect for at that time the wealth of bird-life was terrific.

A wood behind the house called the Spring Coppice was probably the most searched and rewarding. One occasion in particular comes vividly to mind. Having made two or three exceptionally good finds I was completely engrossed in the hunt and had lost all idea of the time. Unbeknown to me my parents had become more and more worried by my failure to return, and finally my father arranged a search with several of the keepers. Eventually I was run to earth. It was somewhere in Morrells Coppice; I forget exactly where, but I do know the following few minutes were painful in the extreme!

Unlike this last decade, which has witnessed a decrease in bird numbers of so many species, cuckoos were numerous. We had sixteen of their eggs in our collection, the majority taken from hedge sparrows, the remainder from robins, wagtails, meadow pipits, and the most unusual one, a nettle creeper (lesser whitethroat).

In later years, it would have been the late Forties, a local shepherd called Fred Morris gave the most perfect imitation of their call that I have ever heard. One evening my son was at his house and was given such a wonderful demonstration that no fewer than six cuckoos were circling the chimney pots, hunting the mimic concealed in a porch. What a delightful character; full of country lore, and with a variety of occupations and hobbies. After saying that, how could he have been anything other than a beekeeper?

For a number of years a cuckoo's egg was laid and hatched in a wagtail's nest in the jasmine porch over our front door. We were never lucky enough to see the actual laying of the egg, whether in the nest or on the ground. Controversy has raged for years as to whether cuckoos lay in the nest or carry the egg to it, but I suspect it could be either way, accessibility of the nest being the deciding factor.

Not surprisingly I was a good climber but got the shock of my young life whilst getting up to a jackdaw's nest hole in a Lombardy poplar. It was high up and I had nearly reached the nest when the wretched tree started swaying. Earlier warnings that it was a very brittle wood which could snap easily came vividly to mind and the sensation was horrible. Each successive sway of the tree felt ever greater and I was too afraid even to move. After what felt like an eternity, it did finally steady, and I thankfully eased myself down just that little bit the wiser!

Once a week two young men, brothers called Gough, came round driving a low dray from which they sold fish. They had a really spanking pony and their time coincided with our walking from school. I believe they really started the trouble, but we were not slow to take it up. They used to shout '*Fish Alivo, Fish Aliv-O*', a ditty which was completed by our shouting '*Four rotten'uns out of Five-O*'.

On this particular day they really did bring out some rotten fish and one of them jumped off the dray and gave chase. I popped through a gate into a grass field. He followed and pounced on me and smacked me round the ears with his stinking fish. My hand came in contact with something soft and I let fly scoring a direct hit in his face. Disaster! It was from something a cow had left behind a little earlier and I was dragged through it, and through it, until mightily distressed.

After that I had to go home, and got there a little late, having spent quite some time at the pool doing my utmost to clean myself up; not that it helped matters, but merely spread it round that much worse! On arriving home I was shooed outside and made to strip off, then into a bath and finally got away with a stiff lecture.

Fights sometimes took place. There was one battle-ground on a triangular piece of grass on the way from school, another one in the cricket field close to the school. It all started around the harmonium where we were practicing for the following Sunday services. Just what it was all about, I really have forgotten, but the challenge was made and accepted.

My opponent was twice my size, and strong, the cricket field the place. I got a terrible tanking and again they were having tea when their very battered son arrived. My father looked at me for some time and then said, 'What have you been doing?' I said 'Fighting'. Again a long searching look and I am sure I saw compassion on his face. He quietly said, 'You will get more sense as you grow older'. How wise he was! Bob Howard and I were friends before the set-to and again afterwards. He was killed in the War; I believe it was on the Somme.

Now a story concerning my brother. Unlike me he suffered relatively little from the cane. This was not altogether by virtue of good behaviour, but rather that he had inherited a great deal of Father's huge physique. From a comparatively early age he towered over the master who was a small man. This created something of a problem and the solution devised was both ingenious, and by the standards of today, somewhat bizarre.

A tall clock tower was the outstanding feature of the school and behind the clock itself there was a small room, or rather a space a few feet square. A vertical wooden ladder gave access to it, and it was up this ladder that Ted was despatched to work in solitary, on the grounds that he 'contaminated' the rest of the class.

The team which triumphed at Worfield.
Norman, centre front.

Norman standing, with
brother Ted.

Ever the opportunist, my brother noticed the speed of the pendulum was controlled by weights on a regulating arm. An inch or so inwards and the old clock fairly began to hammer away. Move them the other way and time dragged. He developed this manipulation to a fine art, forward by day, backward by night. In this of course he had the church clock to assist him and for weeks we kids went home early. Since most local activities were regulated by the school clock in those days the resultant chaos was considerable. No – the culprit never was discovered!

Elections were occasions to look forward to – a holiday as the school was the Polling Station. They were more hilarious affairs than they are today. Nearly everyone wore rosettes. *The Hundred House* did a roaring trade as well!

Candidates on one occasion were Sir Beville Stanier, a Conservative, and Mr Frances Neilson, a Liberal. Practically every school child was there to watch the fun and a man called Clarke from Beckbury appointed himself Major Domo of proceedings. A roadman called Jones was dressed up complete with topper and blue streamers flowing from it. His broom carried as a musket was likewise embellished. All we youngsters, completely under Mr Clarke's influence, sang songs whilst marching around an old elm tree and village stocks outside the school. At intervals he gathered us all around him, telling us tales and asking us riddles. If I can remember the little doggerel we sang, it went something like this:

> *Vote, vote for Beville Stanier*
> *Who's that knocking at the door*
> *If its Neilson and his wife*
> *We will stab them with a knife*
> *For a thousand Shropshire poor*
> *Will not hunger any more*
> *Since the old age pension's on the way*

And there was a lot more of it. That finished, he produced a huge blue rosette and we kids cheered like mad. Then, ever so cunningly, he took a handkerchief from his pocket and from it unwrapped a little china pig which emerged painted red. At that we all yelled Frances Neilson and booed our heads off.

In between whiles, the gent with blue streamers marched up and down with his broom, an old soldier doing musketry drill, and generally acting the clown much to the delight of his audience.

The stocks at Norton. The school gates can be seen background left, and the village pump is just behind the stocks.

3

HIGHWAYS OF THE TREES

Saturday afternoons were without doubt the high spots of the week, for that was when our parents rode into the local town of Bridgnorth by pony and trap. While they were away, activities were governed to a great extent by weather and season but whenever possible they lay outdoors.

Rabbits flourished in huge numbers and afforded sport in various ways. Perhaps our favourite was what we called 'stubbing', the Spring Coppice being the usual venue. Undergrowth was scanty, but there were numerous stubs where trees had decayed giving snug sanctuary to the bunnies. Our spaniel Glen marked if there was one at home and then commanded one of the entrances. Having the longer arm my brother then reached into the cavity and was occasionally able to grip the coney. Usually though we had to resort to puggling with a stick until the occupant bolted, or else crouched and was left. Glen was more than adept at catching the bolters.

Backs of our hands bore evidence of just how strong the kick from a rabbit's leg can be. Those scratches were often deep and most painful. Our best-ever catch was sixteen.

Sometimes we had forays after the squirrels, those lovely red ones which at that time were so plentiful. Both of us were more than useful with a catapult, though in that department I was more consistent than my brother as I practiced more assiduously. Every heap of road stones was searched for the right type of round pebble essential for good marksmanship.

For more serious work we pinched the cartridges used for shooting deer. These were loaded with BB pellets, known as buckshot. A tin held over the fire with pliers was used to melt the lead shot and this was then poured into a bullet mould. We had a bucket of water to hand for cooling the finished product. On one memorable occasion brother Ted accidentally tipped the whole tin of molten lead into it. Results were startling to say the very least! We were mighty lucky to escape with minor damage, but the Harness Room looked a bit of a mess and the bucket no longer held water. An awful lot of explaining was needed on our parents' return!

Back to our squirrel hunt, the purpose of which was not to kill, but to startle the quarry into giving a display of speed and agility which fascinated us. One hunt of well over a hundred yards, with jumps from the outermost branches of one tree to the outermost twigs of its neighbour all made with bewildering certainty, finally ended in a treeless open space. From quite some height he sailed with outspread tail to the ground. Having rushed to cover him with his cap, Ted got well and truly bitten and our little friend was up in the trees again chattering with annoyance and anger. No doubt a practice to condemn, but most enlightening in revealing the squirrels' highways of the woods and the speed at which they can use them.

At harvest time the corn was built into stacks, some of which stood for several months before being threshed. These provided a haven of shelter and unlimited food for the rat population which infested the countryside. When the great day came and the threshing tackle arrived to begin operations, a ring of wire-netting was erected around the stack. A collection of youngsters sporting a great assortment of sticks invariably congregated together with a farm collie or two and the inevitable highly excited terriers.

For long enough it was a waiting game, the odd rat or two showing, perhaps even making a break for it, but it was not until the stack was much reduced and nearing the finish that things really livened up. Terriers chased and snapped bolting rats across the back, killing them instantly with a lightning shake. Glen had a tender mouth which would hardly have disturbed a feather so imagine his surprise when first introduced to this sport. Grabbing a rat he would have retrieved it alive so got well and truly bitten for his efforts; a stern lesson quickly learned! After that he was as smart as the terriers, but with a quick snap across the shoulders and rapid ejection. He never shook them.

As the last few layers of sheaves were reached, the fun and excitement really got going. At that stage the farmhands joined in. It was a case of looking out for yourself as sticks and pykels in brawny arms cleft the air, striking at the rats, usually missing them by inches, but with strength enough to have felled an ox.

Upstairs and then more stairs, were three large attics: an absolute paradise as they were stacked with everything to rejoice the hearts of boys. Initially many of the objects were a mystery to us, but by quizzing our parents and with the help of the old hands we quickly acquainted ourselves with their many varied uses. What a fascinating collection they were.

Nets of every description lined the walls: long-nets and purse-nets for rabbits, together with fishing nets amongst which was an unusual type, ringed with graded cane hoops for use on narrow brooks. In those far away days, trout had been netted in the Worfe during the first few weeks of the season by Reece and Chaplin. This was done two days each week and the catch taken into the Hall. In all this a certain degree of cunning was exercised by the hanging of rabbits over the shallow reaches of the stream which were to be netted. Fish were attracted to those areas by the resultant crop of maggots falling into the water.

There were lengths of stop-netting for pheasants and an

out-sized kind of landing-net with a long wooden handle which was used for catching newly-born fawns. If they can be found during the first few hours of life they are easily caught and at one time castration of a proportion of the males had been practiced on the estate. By doing this herd numbers were maintained with the minimum of culling.

There were 'splungers'. That was the name we knew them by as they were used for 'splunging' along the sides of the Worfe as the draw-net was being worked down to the stop-net. They consisted of a long wooden handle with a circular disc of strong leather nailed to the end. By their use, fish which would otherwise have escaped under the bank edges and in tree roots were moved out into the main current and into the path of the encircling nets.

A large and vicious-looking spear shared a corner with numerous smaller eel spears. At least a dozen shields, beautifully constructed from withy and covered in leather, vied for wall space with the nets. These had been used by keepers both for protection and as seats when watching for poachers. In another corner an old banjo (minus strings) accompanied an assortment of aged and broken-down guns and rifles, bits and pieces, odd stocks and barrels, some of very large calibre.

Alarm guns complete with their boxes of blank ammunition lay in disarray with spool upon spool of the two-strand copper wire used for setting them. Hundredweights, yes hundredweights, of black powder were stacked in seven pound canisters, and cartridge cases for loading a wide range of gauges and sizes were there in hundreds, all interspersed with many calibres of rifle and revolver ammunition. Strong linen bags held shot ranging in size from dust to BB and this disorderly arsenal was rounded off by numerous tins of percussion caps, umpteen bullet moulds of varying size, cartridge loading machines and a wealth of powder and shot flasks.

Amongst it all were twenty-eight pound boxes of yellow sulphur, moulded in lengths of about an inch, and used in the dogs' drinking water. And speaking of dogs, they were well and truly catered for with numerous slip leashes, check collars and muzzles. Many of the latter had undoubtedly been used for coursing greyhounds, but some were huge and must surely have been designed for mastiffs in bygone days.

One of the great prizes were coils of fuse. Some of the old hands told us it had been used mainly for 'stinking' rabbits out of holes prior to shooting days. You can guess the uses boys could put that to. In one attic there were thousands of small 'S' hooks of about an inch. There were also larger ones which could well have been used for hanging game but try as we might, ask whom we would, we never could discover the original use of those small hooks!

Inevitably there were gun-cases, one or two most beautifully made of oak with brass fittings, and some fishing gear most of which was useless. One notable exception was a very heavy brass reel. Perhaps it would have been valuable today for it was certainly of a very early vintage and must have weighed a pound. What a find!

How, one wonders, would modern insurance have reacted to those old attics? Pessimistically no doubt, and probably justified, for some years later a smell of burning was detected in them. Obviously a chimney stack was leaking but several searches over a period of weeks revealed nothing. The smell persisted, the hunt intensified, removal of floor boards, wall panelling, roof tiles all drew blank. Finally it was decided to break into the chimney stack itself, a very large one as the house was extremely old. Removal of bricks allowed a rush of air and a huge beam which lay across the chimney cavity erupted into life and roared away merrily. It must have been quietly smouldering away for a very long time. After that little episode there was some reappraisal of the attics as a storage place!

At one time, probably during the very early days of the old house, the attics had been used as sleeping quarters for some of the keepering staff. A bell was reputed to have hung in the main attic, a rope passing through the floor and into the bedroom below. Doubtless the top floor occupants enjoyed a smoke, and if so, it would be interesting to know just how they came to terms with the powder store.

Before descending those bare oak stairs again I must mention a small window with an ancient butterfly catch. For us lads it afforded a precarious way out onto a long roof ridge. Many a summer's dusk settled on two small figures in pyjamas straddling that ridge. We had discovered that bats lived beneath the tiles in their scores and had perfected a technique for catching them alive as they left for their evening foray. It was great fun but the ground was a long, long way below and I have often wondered just what our parents' reaction would have been had they ever spotted us!

Apley Lodge, home to the Sharpe family 1902–1980

4

RING IN THE NEW

One year my brother and I destroyed thirty-three wasp nests just around the house. Those canisters of black powder came in most useful. Hazel sticks of about eighteen inches were cut: powder was damped sufficiently to knead it onto one end, then covered with paper to retain it on the stick. Finally a good sprinkling of dry powder was tied in with a second covering of paper arranged so that a few inches protruded to put a match to. Stings had little effect on Ted and he took very little notice of them, whereas I dreaded them. However I played my part by holding the hurricane lamp on wasping nights.

After dark there were always a few guard wasps at the entrance hole. A daylight survey was always undertaken to make certain of a sure and quiet approach later that night. Our squib was lit and pushed into the hole as it fizzed; then a sod was quickly dug and rammed down to seal the entrance. Dense fumes were produced by the damp powder and the nest could be dug out a short time later. We used the grubs for fishing.

One famous Saturday afternoon Ted had decided to dig out a strong nest in the Pit Hole. George, the boy at the time, decided to make up the party. We laid a deep circle of damp hay round the nest and soaked it with paraffin. Ted dug like fury as soon as it was lit, heaved the huge comb neatly intact onto the surface, then ran for it. Hours later heavy rain came on and most of the wasps retreated into the comb. Ted collected our father's bee-veil and gloves, together with an empty wooden cartridge box, as he had decided to keep the comb and study them working.

All went well to begin with. George and I watched from a very discreet distance as he carefully, mighty carefully lifted the comb and placed it in the box. He started to carry it up a steep incline, but stumbled half way up, dropped the lot and shouted, 'They're stinging me all over!' We caught up with him in the harness room where he had run to. He had opened the neck of his shirt and was flicking wasps off as they crawled out. One landed in my eye which was soon completely closed.

Ted had stings round his throat, literally by the dozen, and many elsewhere, yet there was no apparent swelling. Some time later a slight swelling did develop and this the doctor diagnosed as goitre. By contrast my final night with the lamp resulted in five stings on my body and what a mess I was in. I have seen Ted stand over a strong nest and destroy it by quietly poring creosote down the hole. In doing so he rarely got stung. Later he kept bees and could take off crates of honey without veil or gloves. Why I should get pipped if I so much as showed my nose round the corner I just cannot think.

Those bees at home were a constant and often very painful menace to me and yet no one was more fond of their honey. Poor old Glen, when only a puppy, was badly stung just going to see their home: yet I have watched the great tits picking them off their alighting board and so far as one could tell the bees never seemed to attack them.

Another great summer pastime was chub shooting in the Severn. On hot days dozens of large chub used to cruise near the surface sucking in the occasional tit-bit and morsel as they floated down. They could be spotted and shot from the high banks with either a .22 rifle or a powerful pump airgun. We quickly discovered the art was to aim low to allow for diffraction. Anyway Glen delighted in swimming out and retrieving the fish which were later boiled for the poultry

Some weeks after we came to Apley, the squire let *The Hundred House* to the Peoples' Refreshment Houses Association. No doubt he believed this would discourage excessive drinking as the landlord was paid a fixed wage, and soft drinks, teas, and coffees were his perks. Old Bob Robinson the 'Pot Boy' of some seventy years was teased and told that in future he would only be able to drink coffee. 'I won't drink their blasted foreign stuff', said he, 'You come round to my place boy an' I'll give thee some real coffee!' Bob had brewed the *Hundred House* beer for many a long year

I can still recall that blue can of barm, perhaps that is not the correct name but the nearest I can think of, being carried past the school and from house to house. It must have been the yeast-like preparation used in the fermentation of the brew. When passing by it gave off a clean, sweet smell, pleasant and refreshing. Beer, good, honest, English beer: yet another country art lost through government controls and taxation.

It would be a pity to miss out the travelling Hurdy Gurdies and the pleasure they gave us children. One swarthy gentleman complete with monkey even used to let us turn the handle of one of these wonderful instruments and what cheery music they churned out!

I wonder if there is still a knife and scissor grinder travelling the roads? That rather primitive contraption visited the village several times a year. It was pedal-driven and operated by a blustering individual, a most likeable soul nonetheless, always with a crowd of youngsters watching him at work

For entertainment, concerts were arranged. Amateur talent flourished and amazingly good a lot of it was. A touring troop, Pear and Boden, also visited us annually. Having spent the summer months on the sands at Rhyll, they toured the villages in the winter. Travelling shows of cine pictures were also held and created intense interest.

Horse-drawn vehicles of every description accounted for most of the traffic through the village. Horses ranged from cobs to ponies and from cart horses to elegant hunters. Teams of six or eight heavy draught horses used for hauling timber frequently passed through, a wonderful sight to see, but the work was cruel and hard. Alty Mapp complete with spear and sword was an impressive figure on his way to compete in the lemon slicing and tent pegging events at the Yeomanry sports. Every week day the Royal Mail arrived at Norton post office at 7am come rain, hail or shine. It was delivered by Mr Teagle, landlord to one of the Bridgnorth pubs, who then drove his horse on to Wellington.

Two horse fairs, the May Day and Luke's were held annually in Bridgnorth. A few years before my time, animals were actually bedded and sold in the High Street. In my day Welsh ponies were still sold on the streets and made a brave sight showing off their paces. How often it rained over the May Fair!

Down the village road, not far beyond the school, the blacksmith's shop was always a great attraction. That ringing, bell-like sound from his anvil could be heard quite some distance away. He used to make a topping hoop for a tanner (sixpence) and all the kids had one.

Stockton Church prides itself on an outstanding peal of bells whilst a leper window recalls days long since gone by. Every New Year's Eve, the ringers, mostly estate workers and men from the farms, went collecting for their year's exertions. A book was carried by the captain of the team in which signed entries of donations were listed. Our house was always the last call, the previous one being Old Park farm from which a walk of one mile across country was necessary to reach us. Needless to say, by the time they arrived the New Year was always well and truly in. Usually they played handbells, perhaps not always in unison, though by that stage it was surprising they could play at all! Anyway, they were grand lads, several of them the sires of sons whose names are perpetuated on the war memorial.

Services were well attended; in fact the church often filled. At Harvest Festivals chairs filled every space and even then many stood in the entrance porch. Each Sunday a trail of people could be seen winding its way up the hill to the church. All the élite came to the morning service and seats were allocated – well at least to the more important citizens. Actually a better term might be graded. The squire, his family and friends were tucked away in a recess front left. Behind them sat a number of the tenants. On the opposite side, front right, sat the rector's family, then the agent's and behind them the hall servants. I can see them all now trooping in, the stately and commanding figure of the housekeeper, rustling skirts sweeping the floor. She shared a pew with the cook and the senior housemaid. Why the remaining maids always arrived in such a rush I could never understand but they were invariably in the deuce of a hurry. All were dressed in black or dark costumes. Attired in morning coat and striped trousers and complete with topper, the butler sat in pew number twenty five. Our family sat behind in pew number twenty six

A spanking carriage and pair with coachman and attendant footman brought the squire and his family to the service. What a contrast in transport. No car, however beautiful, can ever compare with the grandeur and grace of high-stepping horses and an elegant carriage.

My brother and I were stalwarts of the choir. Even now I can recall those sticky cassock pockets where sweets had been left! One funny incident. As the rector was leaving the chancel to deliver his sermon brother Ted released a live mouse he had been keeping in his pocket. Instead of bolting for the nearest dark corner, as we had all anticipated, the mouse trotted behind the parson, turned right when he did and headed up the steps and into the pulpit with him. You can well imagine the effect this had on the choirboys. Complaints about our conduct flowed in. Our beloved schoolmaster was the organist, and because I suffered from that awful complaint of blushing I was pounced on. It can truthfully be said the innocent do indeed suffer for the guilty. On other occasions proceedings were known to have been enlivened by release of a sparrow or bat at appropriate moments.

5

BEARDING THE BILLY

Built in the 1870s, the Home Farm buildings were reputed to be amongst the best in England, timbering of the roofs being a particular feature. Over four hundred acres in extent, the farm took in a further four hundred and sixty acres of parkland, all under the management of Tom Oakley. A great friend to us boys, he was a cricketer in the local team, probably the last one ever to play in it bowling underarm. In doing so he was most successful and claimed many wickets. Some of his deliveries were surprisingly fast. Perhaps the low trajectory had some bearing on his success.

Tom Oakley undertook another important task. Most winters there was a spell of really hard frost which froze the Long Pool. He always tested the ice and when he considered it safe for skating, notified the Hall. Quite a responsibility when you pause to think about it. Anyway we all had tremendous fun with hordes of folk joining in. A fire was always lit on the small island and before leaving for home the ice was swept in readiness for the following evening. On the few occasions the pool has been frozen in recent years, it has been ignored.

At that time the Home Farm staff ran into the teens. A small herd of dairy cows was tended by two cowmen. The Hall staff, farm staff and if I recollect correctly, the gardening staff, all received free milk. We were also fortunate in doing so. Surplus milk was made into butter, the skimmed going to the pigs. Twice a day a youth carried cans of milk and cream, together with baskets of butter, poultry and fresh eggs to the hall. The latter had to be dark brown and have the date stamped on them. During Spring and Summer large numbers of eggs were put into water glass in earthenware steins to be used for cookery during the winter months.

A wooden contraption known as a yoke was used for carrying this somewhat awkward load. It was shaped to fit snugly around the neck and across the shoulders. Chains with hooks dangling from either end supported all the various cans and baskets. Altogether it was a rather comical sight and if encountered on the highway today would certainly slow down the traffic!

We spent hours, especially during the winter time, watching the many activities around those buildings. There was chaff cutting, root slicing, mixing of the food, bedding and feeding of the animals. Naturally enough the stables were a great attraction. Those men loved their horses and following a day's work from six in the morning until six at night frequently returned after supper to clean tack and shine up brasses. How often I have watched five pairs of horses come into the fields fronting our house, breasting the rising ground, heads rising and dipping, gleaming ploughs cleaving the soil, furrows as straight as a die.

No matter the job, whether hedging, ditching, stack building, maintenance, care of the animals, their ability and knowledge was outstanding. And so one could go on and on. Old Woodley the shepherd, the miles he walked. Tom Cooke, there is still Tom's path going over the Long Hill in the park. He lived in the lower lodge a good two miles away. At harvest time he always had a gallon of cider or home-brewed slung over his shoulder, just to see him through the heat of the day.

Frank Abrahams came to work on his penny-farthing

from the village of Sutton Maddock. Then there was Joe Cooke who came on a tricycle; try riding one if you have previously ridden a bicycle. There was Frankie Vaughan the mole catcher. All his traps were home-made, the type with two hoops, horse hair nooses and a long hazel stick for a spring. At that time skins were worth money and were made into clothes for both men and women. Frankie always used the same knife for skinning his moles and cutting up his bread and cheese, change of use marked by a wipe of the blade on his breeches. Quite a character was Frankie, but what a wizard at catching those moles. These were the people I knew and grew up amongst. In all conscience it was hard going for them, yet a happier and more contented crowd it would be difficult to meet.

There was a mule, also a billy goat with a great long beard. At the front of the buildings a section of road was enclosed by gates and railings. I am sure that goat waited for us. If he was on one side of the railings and we the other he invariably edged close enough for us to grab that beard and hang on. Letting go again was the problem for he could clear the gates with ease. Luckily for us he always took a pace or two back before springing and this gave us time to pop through a doorway and into the buildings. He always slept with the cattle for in those days there was a belief that if fire broke out the goat would lead them out to safety.

6

THE INNER MAN

We are all so used to modern amenities that perhaps this is an opportune moment to pause and look back on life as it was lived in my boyhood. No electricity, and few houses had indoor sanitation or baths. Only a few villages enjoyed public transport and that was horse-drawn. There was no National Health Service. Radio was not even dreamed of, let alone television.

Families did not live on tick. Drages were the first firm I can recall advertising credit-selling of furniture. A feature of their promotion was that the goods would be delivered in plain vans! However, to offset all this, the air was clean and sweet and water courses pure and sparkling. Also the countryside was quiet, no flying machines, tractors or chainsaws creating the unholy din of today.

We all derive immense pleasure and satisfaction from food and drink. May I dwell a few moments on the food consumed in our boyhood. Cocoa was a far too prevalent beverage which I heartily disliked. It was usually given as a bedtime drink and we were invariably told it was good for us. One of the first free gifts ever received through coupons was a half pound of Cadbury's chocolates in a floral presentation tin. A year or so ago I gave it a fresh coat of paint and it is still in daily use as a tea caddy, just as it has been for this past sixty years.

A large cooking range incorporating a water boiler on one side and an oven on the opposite was black leaded weekly until it shone again. Its outer edges and also the steel fender were burnished and they really sparkled. Black lead was bought in solid lengths and mixed with water to use as a paste. That old range simply ate fuel, one ton of best coal monthly.

I can still remember that crackling loaf as Mother took it from the oven, holding it to her ear and tapping to see if it was done. A 'Spotted Dick' currant loaf was always baked as well. A week later, loaves from that batch still ate fresh and sweet. No comparison here, there just is none!

For breakfast we always had porridge, bacon and eggs, home-made marmalade and coffee. Shredded wheat was the only cereal I can recall. On Sundays there was always a joint, usually roast beef; a five or six pound cut veined and laced with lines of fat, tender and sweet. In no way is it imagination when the older generation enthuses over the delicious taste of those meals of long ago. Probably the feeding of the animals could have been one reason. I can still see those awkward and heavy bags of cotton cake being carried on the backs of strong men, up the steps and on to the granary floor.

Throughout the seasons, garden vegetables of every description were freshly gathered and cooked. Two great events were the first digging of early potatoes and that first meal of garden peas. Milk puddings galore, jam rolly-pollys, steamed blackcaps, batter, ginger and sponge puddings to mention but a few, the latter always served with golden syrup.

Egg custard was, for that matter still remains, one of my great favourites. They were always made in a container lined with oven-baked pastry. Home-made jams appeared each in their season, so there were always fillings for the range of turnovers, tarts and many varieties of cakes. What expert jam makers they were and the pride they took in making it.

Sunday teas really were teas. Bread and butter, home-made cakes, scones, girdle cakes, sometimes we had Skipper sardines, occasionally a treat of tinned fruit, about the only use the tin opener ever had.

Sunday suppers consisted of the joint eaten cold, served with my mother's home-made green tomato and onion pickle, crusty bread and that never-to-be-forgotten Home Farm butter all washed down with Mr Jones' home brewed. Truly a meal for the gods, usually rounded off with a trifle and how I loved those trifles. Then just to complete a perfect day – cocoa!

For every kind of fruit there seemed to be a wine made locally and mighty good most of it was. That is more than can be said for the cider. A travelling cider press used to visit some of the farms. Some of it really was excellent, but that which qualified for the name of 'Cut Throat' in the local parlance, I could not recommend!

7

NETTING DAYS

Grayling were plentiful in the Worfe and gave good sport during the late summer. There were coarse fish in the stream as well and the estate water was regularly netted to control their numbers. One reason this particular day stands out is that a coracle was brought by someone and no one knew how to use it. That primitive little boat did queer things and got into odd places. It was all rather disappointing for us lads as nobody got tipped out. A good many had a shot at rowing it but it had a bad habit of twiddling round in circles and the frantic efforts to control it with that little wooden paddle only made things so much worse.

For these netting sprees the level of the river was lowered by opening the sluice gates. Someone shouted to one of the keepers who was wading, 'There's a deep hole just in front of you'. 'It's alright I can swim' he replied. 'Show us how'. 'Like this' said he whilst making swimming strokes and bending at the knee. At each dip a trickle of water spilled over the top of his waders. As, no doubt you have already guessed, beer had been freely available at lunch time. Some time later he complained to my father that the new pair of waders leaked!

A real country character much to the fore was old Bob Rodgers complete with eel spear. There he was, splashing through the shallows, as eels drifted down disturbed by the commotion upstream. Try as he might I can not remember him catching a single one. Another character, altogether a different type was a bank manager called Reynolds, reputed to be a good fisherman, as no doubt he was, but why he came armed with a long gaff I have no idea.

After each sweep trout were returned upstream. There were a great many good fish though none topped the two pound mark. When a deepish hole was netted and a really large trout was spotted in front of the draw net there was great excitement; to general consternation he managed to find an opening and escape. All the grayling and coarse fish, mostly roach and a few chub, were carted away to the Severn where they were released. A hundred yards upstream of Rindleford Mill a dozen or so splendid perch, really large ones, and about forty baby pike were taken. The latter were about six inches long and I well recall catching several of similar size when fishing a fly at the overflow.

Getting rid of the pike was the main point of the exercise, but apart from the babies, only five had been caught, four of them about three pounds. Both they and trout are adept at finding sanctuary under banks and ledges, rocks, tree roots, in fact any possible cover whereas the grayling and coarse fish will drop down to the stop net and are that much easier to catch. Even so many do escape.

A final haul in the Mill pool provided the highlight of the day as a really large pike, a monster for the stream, was seen splashing in the net. Excitement was intense. I can still see the bank manager with gaff extended and poised to make a lunge at him if he looked like slipping from the net as it was hauled in. So ended another day to remember, the splungers, the netters and bath carriers all tired out by their day's exertions, not quite as dry as they had arrived in the morning, and the bank manager presented with the great pike – I often wonder whether eaten or in a glass case!

◇◇◇◇◇◇◇◇◇

8

STRANGE BEDFELLOWS

We were extremely fortunate in our father for his knowledge of so many aspects of wildlife was quite exceptional. Through him we learned to appreciate everything around us. His patience was unlimited and he went to endless trouble to show and explain things to us, whatever their nature.

One evening he took me to a fox earth and I was fascinated watching those cubs, inherited instincts a feature of their play, that wily stalk of a pheasant wing or partly-eaten rabbit, the sudden pounce and vicious shake. A fancied alarm and whisking tails disappeared into the earth. After that the stealthy reappearance of first one and then another until the games and fun were once again in full swing. All a prelude and training to the harsher realities of their life ahead. Finally, as the vixen left the earth at dusk, a cub or two tried to follow her. She wheeled round and a snarling yap sent them underground as she loped and faded away.

But that was not the end of the evening, for the highlight was still to come. Just as Father pressed my shoulder to denote that we should go, a badger left the earth, gave an almighty shake and he too shuffled away. Earths are sometimes shared or at least the entrances are. How the living quarters are adjusted I often wonder as their habits are completely contrary. Brock's cleanliness in the home and the fox's couldn't-care-less attitude surely make them the most unusual and unlikely joint householders one could possibly imagine.

In the very near vicinity of an earth with cubs it is common to see rabbits and their young undisturbed and a sitting pheasant hatching a brood. To be quickly away from the earth is the vixen's aim before starting to hunt for the ever-demanding family. I nearly said hungry family but with an abundance of unsavoury remains lying around, hunger seldom enters into it. And what an assortment there can be: rabbits, poultry, game birds, rooks and jackdaws, hares, an occasional lamb, the latter probably picked up dead and the rooks and jacks coinciding with shoots for them. Lambs at times are certainly killed though in lowland areas with normal fox populations this is not the general rule. Many times have I seen the odd cat or two. Their choice of freshly-killed food or carrion is indiscriminate in the extreme.

After cubs are born the dog fox invariably lies up away from the earth during the daytime, sometimes a mile or even more distant. For all that, he is a constant food provider. Those three repeated yaps of the dog heard chiefly when mating and the screeching yell of the vixen are unmistakable. Once in the Park, right at dusk, I watched the dog leave the Terrace and make for the earth. As he drew near he stopped, evidently having winded my scent. I was amazed when he gave a perfect vixen's call, repeating it time after time as he circled well away from the earth. At first I thought I must have made a mistake but as the light finally faded the vixen herself left the earth leaving no doubt as to the sex of the yelling fox. A warning to his mate that all was not well.

It was Jack Leake the second horseman who told me about the otter cubs at Apley Bay. That evening I went there and was well rewarded: a family of three which were about half grown. Fortunately Jack had told me the best approach and where to watch from. I was able to settle unobserved. Soon the cubs were out at play and how they contrasted with fox cubs!

These little chaps were full of the joys of life, sliding and rolling and cascading down the bank; but even at that age always alert to possible danger. One moment there, the next they had gone! I had heard nothing, but the warning sent by the old one had been heard and instantly obeyed. For a long time I remained there hoping they would reappear, but in vain. In fact that was the only time I ever did get the chance to watch that family. News spread, others went to see them and, of course, they moved on.

JOY OF THE DIPPING FLOAT

Leaving our house the road ran a field's length to the Long Pool. How many happy hours we spent there either skating, fishing, bird-nesting, or maybe just climbing trees. There was a variety of fish in it. Numerous carp which we rarely caught; they were much too wary to be deceived by our rather crude methods. We were sometimes successful with them after a thunder storm when the water was discoloured, but even then a catch was indeed rare and we never succeeded in getting one of more than three pounds.

There were large ones. One year an otter visited the pool nightly and killed many of them. It could well have been a family of otters, for they played havoc with the stock. Dead carp lay all round the sides, many good ones, the largest being some ten or twelve pounds. At one end of the pool where it was shallow there was a large patch of bulrushes and in these the carp splashed and rolled, especially on hot days. Jimmie Reece the keeper from Grindle told us that in the winter of the great frost, 1894/5, they were collected by the cart load after the thaw came as the pool had been frozen solid. He also told how the Severn had frozen over as far downstream as Tewkesbury, and how when the thaw finally came, the ice broke up so rapidly that relays of horsemen galloped the length of the river warning people to get off it.

More fun was had with the perch, their size seldom more than four ounces, occasionally a half pounder. Larger ones were prizes indeed! At the deep end of the pool a wall formed its boundary. A few feet out a wooden floodgate was sunk into the water and that was the killing spot. On one occasion we had been catching small ones when my float slid away. I said, 'Here's another,' and gave a real yank. My rod met with heavy resistance. A huge perch rolled on the surface and was off. That was tragedy indeed. He would most likely have broken my tackle anyway for as he rolled over he exposed a depth and length of body which has haunted me ever since!

Shoals of very small roach darkened the surface on hot sunny days. Even a bird passing over skedaddled them into a frenzy of fright and down into the depths they went; soon to reform again and resume their sunbathing until the next disturbance. We made bread paste and using morsels of it on tiny hooks caught them by the dozen.

Tench grew to a reasonable size, one-to-two pounds being the usual weight. Larger ones were never caught, also very few less than a pound. They are one of the finest fish in the so-called coarse fish category, game fighters and beautiful to look at. A close humid evening is probably the best time to take them. Their habit of blowing bubbles was often their undoing. A nice fat lobworm dropped into the ring of surface bubbles was often successful. Being slow takers the float usually twitched for quite a time, but they have a habit of rising with the bait in their mouths indicated by the float flattening out on the surface and that was the time to tighten.

Those marvellous May evenings of which we seem to get so few now. King Sol sinking behind Caughley to the west, promise of renewal of life in the green of the fields, trees newly leafed in shades innumerable, the excitement and activity of all creatures but a prelude to what is to follow. There is always the waterhen bobbing across the water, its white tail feathers flipping up with each chug along. A somewhat quarrelsome bird with so many different voices, when angry harsh and strident: a bird that

Jimmie Reece alongside the deer fence bounding Morrels.

flies high at night with infrequent cry of somewhat eerie nature. A brood of young ducks only a few days old, enjoying their evening meal, their movements like streaks. They almost look as if they are blown here and there, how their little legs must move, but each dart a tasty morsel of midge hatching out.

Coots always seem to be squabbling but when feeding the ring of water from their dive can be so deceptively like that of a rising trout. When surfacing they seem to just bob straight up out of the water. Always a few little grebes, 'dab-chicks', which upend and disappear so quickly, resurfacing a few yards away, or maybe many distant ones. A heron skims over the tall trees and glides down to land on the log sticking out from the water; there for a moment, then a speedy retreat as one is spotted.

Water voles, delightful little animals, always busy swimming either from here to there, or from there to here. I guess always a reason and object in their comings and goings. A stock dove which breasts the water to drink, the wagtail at the cow drink, chaffinches, flycatchers and a host of others all dining out on the masses of water flies hatching out. Nor could one leave out Jenny Wren hunting every chink and crevice of wall and tree trunk, neither the robin. One always turns up from somewhere. Sometimes a hare lopes along, often stopping close by with twitching whiskers and always a puzzled expression, then away with a burst of speed as she realises things are not what they ought to be.

A scolding blackbird, then a glimpse of brown, gone only to reappear again, white front and black tail now leaving no doubt as to its species. A born hunter. To watch one is a lesson in dedication, the cursing birds distracting not one iota from the work in hand. Today the stoat population is at a much lower level than years ago. Overhead the gentle rustle of leaves, disturbed by a puff of wind which fades and goes no-one knows where. Not so the big aspen just beyond the cow drink. Its leaves are never still, but shiver all the time, the wood the Cross was made from, it is said.

The swallow tribe flip the water moistening mud to make their nests. And from a distance that most arresting sound, the plover's mating song, each sweet note timed it would seem to each flashing wing beat of the wheeling bird. Skylarks spiralling up into the sky with delighted song, then their descent a drift and stop, a drift and stop, the final sudden plunge and miraculous pull up and dainty landing. All this and the joy of the rod and dipping float. Who could ask for more!

◇◇◇◇◇◇◇◇

10

CORACLE MEN

The Ironbridge coracle men were truly amazing in the making, handling and uses to which they put their small craft. Many a time I watched them laying their eel lines, nearly always fishing in pairs, long lengths of line with suspended hooks baited with worm or small fish, bleak, gudgeon, loach, and minnow all used, the lines weighted with stones or bricks at each end.

This took place in the evening and if you wished to see them lifted you had to be there at daylight next morning. If left until later, the eels snarled the lines into an entangled mess though they would have lain quietly enough during the hours of darkness. Drifting down the river the previous evening the coracle men would have laid a great number of lines, selecting the spots to drop them in and covering a distance of some miles. Even now I am still mystified as to how those positions were marked. It could have been by memorising the river bank formations, bushes, rocks, inlets and so on, yet I cannot convince myself that was the full explanation. Those men were so river-wise that I really believe it was an instinctive reading of the element that in a way was a part of them.

I do know what was certain. One reach down with a boathook and those lines were lifted the next morning without hesitation and with absolute certainty; the squirming catch coming over the side and into the coracles. Drifting down from line to line until the final one was lifted, it was a truly amazing feat of observation and memory.

They also netted for coarse fish, often lifting their coracles at Linley and going home by train. Officially they were prohibited from netting for sixty yards above a ford and throughout its length but how many times did I watch them do just that! It was not coarse fish they made their beer money with. Trout and salmon, yes!

Of course they were notorious poachers, but I am not going into that aspect of the lives of the Ironbridge coracle men. So much has been written about them already. This I do know, they were an almighty headache for every gamekeeper within a radius of many miles. Eustace Rodgers is probably the last of these remarkable men. He has been heard many times on the BBC.

11

FROM LINLEY TO BRIDGNORTH

Daily train journeys to Bridgnorth were full of interest. On the way to the station there was the river to cross, always a great stopping place, though never in the mornings! Looking down into the water, shoals of fish were to be seen cruising around, and up and down. Mostly chub, some nice fat ones amongst them, making the occasional dimple as a rising fish sucked a fly from the skin of the surface. Frequently I amused myself dropping fragments of grass stem, or better still the ends of fern fronds which are heavier. When lucky enough to drop on the water near a fish they were usually accepted but the subsequent ejection was so fast it was so easily missed. Propelled by a good old puff, it shot several inches out of the fish's mouth.

Occasionally a salmon splashed at the rocks above the boathouse some distance upstream. A small brook rising from the Willey Pools entered the river almost under the bridge. Crevices in the walls of the culvert through which it made its final dash to the Severn were favourite nesting places of dipper and water wagtail.

From Linley station the first part of the journey took us through woodland. In springtime a wealth of wild flowers lined the route, banks yellow with primrose and cowslip, then the delicate anemone to be followed by the massed colour of bluebells and the white garlic of the Rookery.

Later the undergrowth became dense and individual species no longer displayed with such telling effect. Only the taller varieties were still distinguishable from the moving train, herb willow and foxgloves standing out in colourful formation. Chestnut Coppice is rightly named, as heavy crops of chestnuts provided an abundance of food for hosts of birds and animals, besides quantities gathered by many folk.

Snug, warm and basin-shaped, well and truly sheltered from the elements, Chestnut Coppice was a favoured winter roosting place for wood pigeons. In the autumn vast hordes of migratory birds augmented our own woodies. A broad opening extended from the middle of the coppice down to the railway line. From the passing train hundreds upon hundreds of their dark forms were to be seen in tall timber silhouetted against the remaining daylight in the western sky.

The old ferry and its successor at Linley. Spring Coppice in the background

51

Winter floods can be rather frightening on the Severn and from the carriage windows one used to see a complete transformation. Flood water covered the fields on either side of the train as it chugged along on its raised elevation. At such times the flooded valley presents a truly amazing picture when viewed from the Castle Hill in Bridgnorth. As the floods subsided, immense activity was to be seen amongst the birdlife. For them it was a bonanza of food with water fowl and gulls collecting on the shrinking patches of shallow water. All the surrounding sodden land was alive with birds by the hundred, plover, fieldfares, redwings, wagtails, thrush and blackbird with, needless to say, hordes of starlings predominating. Most noticeable of all amongst that feathered host was the heron's soldierly stride, pausing, peering, then striking like lightning with that long spear-like bill of his.

12

THE BIG STICK

A group of keepers were night watching near the junction of Mapp's lane with the main road. They had a new recruit . A young fellow named Bert had joined the force and had come armed with a very large stick. One or two of the old hands suggested he should perhaps have brought his mother, ' Just to be on the safe side!'

Time passed and they heard a horse and trap rattling along the main road towards them. It had been Market Day in Bridgnorth and they knew exactly who it was. A very drunken farmer was sleeping it off in the back of the trap whilst the horse found his own way home.

By way of a little light diversion one of the keepers stepped into the road and turned the old nag down Mapp's Lane. Away he trotted and noise from his progress gradually faded away. Some time later he could be heard coming back again and by that time his passenger was beginning to show a little interest in proceedings. Time and again he kept complaining, 'I can undershtand you going down there you old fool, but 'ow in 'ell you got turned round, thatsh what I canner undershtand!'

Later that night they came across another diversion. Three of the Ironbridge laddies who decided to run for it. It turned out that apart from having a big stick the new recruit could also run a bit and he quickly left the older fellows behind. Following in the wake of the chase they came across a body. A few score yards further on there was a second body and the chase was still on ahead of them. Finally they caught up with Bert and the third poacher.

It was a long, long time before the bodies showed any signs of recovery. The old hands had well and truly got the wind up for it looked very much as though the new boy had inflicted really serious damage. Fortunately that proved not to be the case but rest assured, Bert carried a lighter weapon after that!

13

◇◇◇◇◇◇◇◇◇

HOT CINDERS

After leaving the village school my parents had been planning to send me on to Bridgnorth for a couple of years but the agent, W.O. Wilson, asked them if I would go into the Estate office instead. I simply leapt at the chance: anything to get away from that wretched school! So, next day, my father went with me to the Estate Office. On the following Monday, at the age of fourteen, I started work with John Overton to whom I became greatly attached, also his wife Clara. To me they were a wonderful couple.

With one notable exception the routine at the office was so very similar from day to day. On alternate Mondays my duty was to go collecting rent from the cottage tenants in the town. As a result I knew every single corner of Bridgnorth and a great many of its people. There were times when I found it more than embarrassing, yet learned a great deal of the ways of many folk and how they lived. Many left the rent book and cash on a table. This I used to sign for and frequently did not see the owners for several visits. Few rents exceeded half a crown (12½p) a week. Many were in arrears and owed substantial amounts. Rent books were reviewed annually and all those in the clear were allowed a fortnight's rent.

Most houses were spotless, in fact shiningly clean, others not so spotless, but the majority were delightful people and a pleasure to know. A sprinkling of the rougher element, the last of the bargees, lived in a street called The Cartway. They were all well on in years and with mighty interesting experiences to relate. Suffice to say their lives had been hard and very, very fast!

Those years spent at the office were happy ones, but made only so I believe by the freedom of country pursuits not denied me, and the kindness of both the agent and the Overtons. Office work did not appeal and I knew it was really not my niche in life. The train on which I used to come home left Bridgnorth at four o'clock. There was a bridge for crossing the lines and the usual notice warning passengers not to do so other than by said bridge. Very often I just made it by the skin of my teeth and frequently hopped down and did exactly what the notice expressly forbade. On this particular day I was carrying two parcels I had been asked to bring out for a neighbour. One of them was a lady's hat.

Just as I was passing behind a stationary goods train it was suddenly shunted by the engine and pushed me over between the lines. My shoulder and arm were across one of the rails and I whipped them away just in the nick of time Then followed the alarming sensation of the clanking trucks passing over me. Many a time I had noticed the long couplings hanging down and now wondered if they would hit me, worse still the hot cinders dropping from the fire box.

Soon a porter was kneeling on the edge of the platform close to me and shouting, 'Lie still! Lie still!' Needless to say this was all at the top of his voice and I bet he never knew where I wished him as everyone's attention was being attracted. As bad luck would have it, it was a Monday, auction day, and the station was simply packed.

Next morning I was escorted to the station master's office, a spruce important little man who congratulated me on being alive and then gave me a heck of a telling off. At that age I was extremely self conscious and I am sure that following week was quite the worst of my life. In the street people would look at me and then turn and speak to each other. 'There's that young fool the train went over,' I could imagine them saying.

Walking home through the wood the following Thursday I came face to face with a railway inspector who had been to see my parents. Strangely enough no one had mentioned it to them and, stupidly perhaps, I had not done so either. He was a tall, bearded, kindly-looking man. He said his visit was a serious one as the Company was thinking of prosecuting. Some years earlier a clergyman's son had been killed doing exactly the same thing. My only explanation was that being very pushed for time I was afraid of missing the train. A week later a letter was received saying that after reading his report the Company had decided not to prosecute and God bless him for that!

On Thursdays the rector frequently arranged to fish the Higford stretch of the Worfe. At that time the half day holiday in the town also fell on Thursday. He used to commence fishing in the early afternoon and when I arrived at Linley station there was a pony and trap waiting to take me over to join him.

On the day in question things had been very quiet and we had taken an early tea at the Mill House at Higford. Afterwards a great evening's sport was enjoyed and we were sitting down having a rest. A good fish rose under the near bank and I called his attention to it. I suspect he was somewhat tired, but as the fish moved again I could not refrain from saying ' There he is'. To my joy he said 'You have a try for him.' That was the best fish of the day and weighed one and a half pounds. Later on I had another session and caught two more good ones. After eating a superb salmon supper later that evening, I was given all three to take home. Now that was a day to remember!

He was a great friend to me and a year or so later was going to take me with him for a month's fishing on Loch Shin in Sutherlandshire. Alas it was never to be as he suffered a heart attack and died a few weeks later. During those weeks I went to visit him every Tuesday and Friday. Mrs Noel-Hill later told my mother that during those weeks he had looked forward to my coming more than anything else. He left me his Armstrong split-cane fly rod, a reel and a cast case. I still have the reel and cast case.

During my days at the office I frequently obtained a permit to fish the Worfe from the agent. He was sometimes a little on the gruff side and on occasion I was said to be a nuisance, but somehow I was always granted permission. Most frequently the beat fished started at the Towns Mills (also known as Fort Pendlestone) and extended upstream and beyond Rindleford Mill to our boundary some distance beyond the old Burcote Mill.

Old Knowles the miller, followed by Grainger and Powell were all masters of their trade, now of course gone for ever. More's the pity! Bread from flour ground by large round stones so skilfully fashioned was something to remember, in fact impossible to forget. My mother used to buy a sack of Canadian wheat which was then sent to Rindleford for grinding. Flour was stored in a large round tin container housed in a corner of the kitchen. Wheaten flour with no additives, bread crisp and nutty, clean and wholesome

Upstream from Rindleford the valley narrowed, its sides densely timbered, high and rugged with sandstone outcrops. It was one of the most pleasant places in a valley of great beauty. Rich in bird life, it was the home of kingfisher, water ousel, sandpiper and at times one could be flustered nearly as greatly as the wild duck herself as she flayed the water with mock damaged wing to draw you away from her young. Sometimes the nightingale's song could be picked out from the music of so many other songsters.

But to return to the Thursday afternoon in question. It was probably the first occasion I had ever fished the beat and despite my initial success at Higford, I was very, very inexperienced. By the end of the day I had much to ponder on and how often in later life I wished it were possible to have fished that afternoon and evening over again. It was quite perfect weather, either the last few days of May, or the first week in June. Fish were rising with that exciting plop, a sound sufficient to attract attention and even be heard from around the next bend in the river. Not difficult to guess the mayfly was well and truly up.

Three mayflies had been bought in the town the previous day. Large in size, they were dyed a brilliant yellow, mallard feathers formed the wings, raffia the bodies and whilst being cast they sounded like humming birds in the air.

The fish I put down that day! It is no exaggeration to say I have never seen so many good fish since; some were really large ones, absolute beauties. By the time I had fished up to Rindleford I had caught two smallish trout and a grayling. Worse still my stock of mayflies was expended. One was in a fish. My fly having dropped pretty well on his nose he grabbed it as it hit the water. Alas, I struck too hard and left the fly in him. How easily done! Another resided in an overhanging bush on the far side of the river; the third and last, despite a desperate search, I had somehow just managed to lose. Finally I made my way to a cottage where I had tea and afterwards dropped back to the Worfe bridge and fished up to the mill again. Several small flies were tried and ignored until I finally put on an alder and caught one or two decent fish which somewhat redeemed the disappointment of the day.

The Worfe was never an easy river to fish. Though the banks were low and the water easily enough covered, its trout were extremely shy. As I grew more experienced and more successful the lessons of that first day were well and truly learned; naturally not in one day but over a period of time. They were never to hurry to cast to a rising fish, but rather to study the approach and place to cast from, to keenly scrutinise the flow of water so as to avoid possible drag and never forget to make sure the back cast is free of obstructions.

A sizeable patch of the outfield on the Apley cricket ground was always mown and rolled for the boys and what great games we enjoyed. To graduate into the mens' team was every lad's ambition and I was an established member by the age of thirteen. Matches were played on Saturday afternoons, our opponents being drawn from the surrounding villages and local towns. Within a radius of five miles we made our own way to matches, otherwise it was horse transport. For some distant matches such as Burwarton it was a case of walking much of the way for the road was very hilly. At the foot of each one we all left the brake and walked in order to ease the horses.

After beginning work at the estate office I soon became a regular member of the Bridgnorth Thursday XI and on a number of occasions I was fortunate to play in country house games, usually travelling to them with W.O. Wilson the agent. These were day matches, the excellent lunches and teas laid on a feature fondly recalled. Sir Raymond Tyrrwhit of Stanley Hall used to bring a team up from Leicestershire where he had a hunting lodge. On one occasion Gillie Ratcliffe, a fine young cricketer who was employed in the Hall gardens, was called over by Sir Raymond as he was walking out to bat. Things were not going any too well at the time and he told Gillie he would give him a shilling for every run he made. Later in the day Gillie returned with a not out score of fifty two and collected Lord only knows how many weeks wages!

Just how it all came about eludes me but I was invited to fish Sir Raymond Tyrrwhit's pools in a little screened-off beauty spot known as The Dingle. They were stocked with rainbows and that was the first time I ever fished for them. Sir Raymond came down and I asked him if I could leave some at the Hall. He said not to do so as he could always go down and catch them as he wanted. He then said he was considering buying a new rod and asked what I thought would be suitable. I suggested he purchase one from Hardy's. 'Come again next Saturday afternoon and pick the one you consider best. Bring Hardy's catalogue with you.'

This I did and he again joined me at the waterside. After a very cursory glance at the catalogue he said he would order the one I had suggested. Then he asked me how many fish I had retained the previous week. I told him a brace. 'Well today take one for each member of your family.' The following Thursday he brought down a lovely split cane rod, 'The Selected One', a new reel and line and said I had better try it out and pass opinion as to its suitability.

He was a quite amazing man, a bachelor and as by now you have probably guessed, somewhat eccentric! Albert Fulcher, his sub-agent, told me it was very doubtful if he would ever use the rod. If he did so it would most certainly be for only a few minutes and on his return to the Hall would send someone to collect it.

Though he did not shoot himself Sir Raymond reared several hundred pheasants. His woods were ideally situated and capable of giving first-class shooting. He was also something of a showman. When in residence he visited the town daily, always in the mornings and at about the same time, a pony and trap one day, a tandem the next and maybe a carriage and pair the following, always with mettlesome, beautifully groomed horses and immaculate conveyances.

A commanding figure, the long cigar was never absent as he rattled through the North Gate and down the High Street finally pulling up outside the Post Office. Believe it or not a clerk used to come out and attend to his wants. The cigar more often than not a dummy!

It was after I had learned to shoot. Cartridges were only a few shillings a hundred, and there was so much to shoot at, rabbits and pigeons being the main quarry. One afternoon I was sent rabbiting across the Old Park farm. It was the very end of the shooting season and for some reason a brace of partridges was required. Father had told me to shoot them if the opportunity arose. As I was walking along the road known as Mapp's Lane a covey swung over me very high and very fast. I took a brace out of them as clean as a whistle, my first right and left at partridges.

Old Park farm was a frequent port of call. Old Mrs Mapp was a delightful lady, kind and generous. The Mapp family are the oldest farm tenants on the estate, their grandsons still carrying on the tradition. One day Mrs Mapp told me the new curate had called to see her. Asked what he was like she replied, 'He's rather like a chip in milk.' That is the only time I ever heard that expression, but how very expressive.

She was also weather-wise in an unusual way. If she said 'The well is drawing' it was for fine weather, but if the well was not drawing it would rain. When drawing, there was a distinct humming noise emitted. Take it from me, that old well seldom got it wrong.

Partridge shooting at that time really did commence on the first of September. Driving was not so popular as it was to become in later years and walking up was the order of the day. Whilst it did not demand so expert a degree of marksmanship from the guns, the opportunities it provided for the dogs to exhibit their skills were legion

Partridge shooting days gave W.H. Foster great scope to inspect the estate. He greatly enjoyed days with Tom Oakley, my father and himself shooting. These were known as 'bye' days. One day on the Home Farm he stopped the line and said 'Oakley go and have a look at that gate'. Not the best of starts to the day as the gate collapsed on being touched and out came his little book. From then on there were many delays as every near gate had to be inspected and I bet a pound Tom Oakley did not lean his weight on any others he examined that day.

At every possible opportunity I joined them on shooting

A meet pre-1914 style. No cars, no labradors, but plenty of flats and curlies

days, if only for the last hour or so. On one particular occasion I was able to spend the whole day with them. They met at the Old Park farm. The squire, a visiting guest or two and my father comprised the team. After a long discussion operations commenced. Stubbles were walked towards a large field of mixed roots which at that time would have been mangolds or swedes.

A covey or two lifted and settled in the root field and there were several shots at hares. A good line was formed and the roots walked. Several partridges were shot and collected. Then suddenly the air seemed full of birds with shots ringing out all down the line. I counted five fall, but after only four had been picked up the line again began to move on. I said that there was another one and the search resumed with dogs working all over the place. As time passed with no result there were remarks from one or two of the keepers that they were quite certain only four birds had been shot. My father called me and asked if I was quite certain I had seen five fall. I replied, 'Yes, one was a long way out, nearly a hundred yards away.' By this time the squire was becoming irritable and also questioned me and as you may guess I was getting a little red in the face.

All except my father were convinced I had made a mistake. Father got his dog well out and at last he struck a line and worked it right to the far end of the field. Twice we saw a bird jump up in front of the working dog; several times he checked and cast cleverly to regain contact. Right in the very corner of the field, some two hundred yards from where we were standing he gathered the partridge. A great demonstration and a quite remarkable retrieve. The squire's irritation vanished and he congratulated me, but human nature being what it is he then chided everyone else for not having observed it! Perhaps I have made a longish tale of this, but then the dog was dear old Glen. God bless him.

14

SWAN SONG

Apley Park was alive with rabbits and in late autumn when bracken was dying down a lot of fun was enjoyed. Clear areas between narrow strips of bracken made ideal stands to shoot from. Glen excelled at this type of work and was adept at bringing the rabbits to the waiting gun. He took a wide cast out and then hunted back towards you. On hearing a shot he charged out of the cover, and provided the rabbit was dead took another cast back into the bracken and hunted it up again. Needless to say this state of perfection was only attained after long practice. Hunt ended, he set to and retrieved the dead rabbits.

Sometimes rabbits were left to be collected later for a game bag being filled as they are shot soon becomes very heavy. On a hot summer's day any lessening of the load is appreciated so they were frequently hidden in undergrowth or bracken. Glen could remember where they lay and go straight to them, no matter how much time had elapsed. When left with game or rabbits he remained any length of time and you may be assured no one ever took them from him.

One afternoon my brother and Harry Marshall were sent to ferret the Long Hill. Until he considered we could shoot well enough, my father insisted we only loaded with one cartridge. There was much to be said for the practice, also points against. Anyway Ted was still 'on probation', but the conies were bolting well and temptation proved too great.

Father had evidently made a point of spending the afternoon nicely within earshot and on his return Ted was greeted with 'What on earth have you been shooting at? Fifty three shots and a lot of them doubles' As an afterthought and much to brother Ted's relief, 'Anyway, how many did you get?' 'Forty six,' replied Ted. On that hillside liberally dotted with large anthills, that was some going and he was somewhat proud of his performance. 'Just as I said, just as I said! Shooting and blasting away. You'll never make a shot!'

On another occasion Ted was sent into the park to shoot a buck with great emphasis that one, and one only, had to be shot. After much walking he finally came up with a small group, their antlers just discernible above the tall bracken on a little mound known as Spion Kop. He was able to approach within close range without being spotted. High bracken screening the animals only gave an occasional glimpse and chance of a shot which was finally taken.

The bunch broke and scattered but were not moved any distance. That first shot had been difficult and uncertain. Ted thought he had missed and quickly a second shot was fired. Even then, though they again broke and scattered, the animals did not leave the bracken. Again, perhaps foolishly, yet another shot was taken, this time with the certainty of a kill. To his great consternation three prime bucks lay dead and ahead of him a little explaining!

Of course the reason the animals had not charged away after the first shot was their uncertainty of the direction the shot came from. I saw similar incidents on several subsequent occasions.

In the middle reaches which I fished, the Severn was never a really good trout stream. Wading was discouraged, so I kept an old pair of nailed boots tucked and hidden beneath a stub, and waded with turned up trousers and bare legs which looked a little on the blue side when the water was cold.

The *Fishing Gazette* was handed on to me by the Reverend Noel-Hill and I read everything else I could lay hands on. My aim was to be the purest of the pure so only fished a dry fly. Looking back what an awful lot I missed by doing so. In later years I knew that the derisive and disparaging stigma attached to the wet fly referred to at that period as 'the chuck and chance it method' was altogether wrong. Even so I still firmly believe the dry fly to be the most enjoyable form of fishing there is.

Some lovely pools, often at the draw of the throat, usually held good fish; and shallows over the gravel beds could be rewarding. Deep water, difficult without a boat, probably held the best fish though few and far between. Percy Price in the summer of 1921 caught twenty-three of two pounds or more by what he termed fishing the willows. Low branches sweeping out from the base of the bush and across the stream diverted and accelerated the flow of the current, so guiding all the choice mouthfuls a feeding

The Severn in the 1920s. Note the low branches
diverting the flow of the current

trout would welcome and receive with the minimum of effort. Chub abounded and many large ones were caught when fishing these lies.

Success depended so much on the skill of the rower. Being both an excellent fisherman and boatman, his friend Bern Turner was the perfect companion. Bern did most of the rowing, in fact nearly all of it, for Percy had been badly gassed in the trenches a few years earlier and died prematurely from the effects.

April, if mild and warm, followed by May and June were the best months. After that, shoals of coarse fish fry replaced the surface-feeding of the trout. It was always possible to take a brace or two of sizeable fish in the evening following a warm sunny day. My best catch ever was four brace and I never caught one of two pounds, the average weight being about three-quarters. My best-ever night was at Brights, only three, but beauties all just under the two pound mark.

Odd grayling were sometimes taken and the enormous shoals of dace were great fun taken on a dry fly. They rose in scores and what perfect practice they gave a youngster in that most difficult art known as striking. Chub also gave good sport. They could be caught in the runs, but it was also highly instructive to dap for them off the high banks of the deeper water. A deal of craft was needed as one false move, it could even be the shadow of the rod, and they faded away into the depths.

By comparison with the conditions of today the keeper's life was hard, yet at that time they were looked upon as normal and in no way a hardship. When the Hermitage farm was shot over, Reece the keeper from the Grindle beat walked eight or nine miles to get there. After goodness knows how many more miles walked during the day there was the return trip. I can still see Jimmy now, wishing everyone 'Goodnight' and setting off with his retriever Sailor; a strong good man full of dry humour and a great friend to us boys.

In wet weather and on dewy mornings there was the certainty of a soaking and the discomfort that went with it. If only around the feet and legs, one was thankful. They were a hardy race though and it was infra dig to wear great coats. Today a great range of water-resistant clothing adds greatly to a day's enjoyment.

At the conclusion of an early morning's cubbing, the huntsman, Pittaway, was calling out his pack. He had a beautiful voice with an amazing range and variety of calls. On this particular none-too-successful occasion he was carolling in a ringing high-pitched tone, 'And where the hell are we now?' The squire said to Father, 'What does he say?' There was no need to answer for again it rang out sweet and clear. 'And where the hell are we now?' 'I'll just go and tell him,' said the squire.

Hunting took pride of place in W.H. Foster's life. At that time a private telephone connected the hall with various heads of departments and after a day's hunting he invariably rang up my father to discuss, frequently at great length, all its happenings and details.

On two successive occasions The Terrace had been drawn blank. You may be assured that was a very serious matter. At Belle View there was a large break of briars and Father suggested that next time he should bring his spaniels and hunt it out after the pack had been through it. This was agreed. Glen and a Welsh spaniel were put in to the accompaniment of the squire cracking his whip, their combined effort springing a brace of foxes which went away in full view. The really amazing thing was Father was instructed to take his 'pack' and hunt the briars on all subsequent visits of the hunt. Believe me those spaniels seldom failed to find though I suspect they were less than popular with the hunt staff.

From October to the following April, the period covering the hunting season, no barbed wire was allowed to be used anywhere on the estate. That this was possible testified to the

A meet in Apley Park

perfection of the hedgerows and fences. Prizes were awarded for the best-kept farms and great pride was taken in the fencing of fields. On every farm an outstanding hedge-layer was employed. Tom Oliver from Astol Farm, Joe Cooke from the Home Farm, to name but two, excelled in their craft and skill. Fencing materials and live quick (hawthorn) were for free from the estate yard and the nursery.

The Reverend Noel-Hill had taken a shoot in partnership with a nephew called Jack. That was soon after I had left school. One day, the rector's son Michael, who was about my age, made up the party with myself and Glen. We travelled from Linley station, changing at Buildwas for Wenlock, where a pony and trap was waiting to convey us to the farm we were to shoot over. It was a large, well-kept area of mixed crops. Two or three stubbles were walked in towards a field of roots. Then a field of seeds was walked and as we had only seen one pair of old birds the odd remark was passed that things were not looking too promising. A decision was taken to try the seed clover and then things did happen. Several really good coveys were found and well broken up, some going into the roots. More coveys were found in the roots and the bag began to assume very happy proportions. With skilful driving-in from outlying stubbles and grasses, the clover and roots gave the two guns more excellent shooting.

Glen was in his usual position between myself and the next in line. When root fields were being walked he got away with a bad habit. Instead of keeping to heel he placed himself between my father and the next person. He was so persistent in this that finally it was accepted, the view being taken that when tight to heel the human scent foiled, to however small a degree, the scenting ability of the dog. Whatever it was he still contributed to the bag with the bunnies he whipped off their seats. At that he was great. A mark, then a curve of the body and dive in, all in one movement. Rarely did he fail!

To my joy he worked perfectly, gaining a great measure of praise from the two sportsmen. The bag I forget precisely, but it was in the forty brace bracket. It was a glorious September day, the shooting was first class and I am certain that every bird shot was collected. I know that everyone was delighted with the day.

One Friday evening we were at cricket practice. At least we were going through the motions, for everyone's eyes and ears were attuned to catching sight or sound of their first flying machine. It was the occasion of the *Daily Mail's* £10,000 flying contest from Manchester to Bristol. The year, I think, was 1911. For most of the day we had been listening and scanning the skies.

At about seven that evening we heard a distant drone and it was quite some time before the flying machine came into view looking not much bigger than a bumble bee. It took long enough passing over us and finally disappeared over the horizon. Noise from its staccato engine was so unlike the powerful roar of the present day machines.

Next day another machine landed for repairs in a field south of Madeley. Its pilot was called Valentine. Crowds of people journeyed to see it and the following night we had the pleasure of watching it take off. Everyone's heart was in their mouth as it cleared the field's fence by a mere whisker. 'Pop' Jones from Bridgnorth had done a roaring trade selling his drinks. He even had to make a second journey for a further supply which again sold like hotcakes. But then 'Pop' never did miss a trick!

That machine appeared terribly fragile. Its wire struts and indeed the whole construction looked mighty unsafe to me. Those early airmen must have had great courage. At Beckbury, some three miles away, Colonel Cody went over in his 'Flying Circus', a machine looking like a box-kite. A Frenchman won the race. If memory serves correctly his name was Vedrines. Another Frenchman was in at the kill and there was a mix-up when landing. One of them came down on the wrong ground and had to take off again and make the correct one.

Of course I can only speak of country life, but working conditions were to some extent improving. Although the motive power was still the horse, mechanisation was coming more and more into its own. One evening Tom Oakley brought a new

Valentine's flying machine is admired at Madeley. As Norman writes:
'Those early airmen must have had great courage.'

machine into the freshly-cut field of hay in front of Apley Lodge. It was a tedder for turning the crop and the picturesque line of workers raking it into rows was soon a forgotten feature of that time.

So too the binder had taken over from the scythe. The only task awaiting the scythe now was preparing the field for the binder to work. How often I watched Tom Cooke and Bill Sargeant come into a cornfield early in the morning to open it out for the binder. At the gateway a patch was cut for the binder to come in and set up. Then a road was cut right round the field, one mowing, the other collecting and tying into sheaves with bands of straw, the job being finished ready for the binder to work after breakfast. The swan-song of the rake and scythe.

Those years leading up to the Great War at the beginning of the century I recall as good ones. Of course I can only speak of the countryside where working conditions had slightly improved, though wages were still low and the hours worked far too long. In both home and workplace so many labour-saving devices and machines we now enjoy and take for granted were unknown, in fact undreamed-of. Yet even so, people of my generation will confirm they were good years and their faces still light up with the memory of them.

There was a contentment and certainty in the way of life for all sections of the community which has never been recaptured.

In having so much to enjoy I count myself fortunate in the extreme. Things of interest, often great interest, were happening all the time. Never a dull moment!

15

◇◇◇◇◇◇◇◇◇

SPRING 'WOODIES'

After the Great War I came home to another spaniel, Jess, a grand-daughter of Glen. She was full of the joys of life, friendly and affectionate, tireless, no day too long. I can see her now stretched out on the hearth in front of a blazing log fire after a day's shoot. A slight twitch of the toes, forepaws coming into play, then squeaky little grunts until her whole body was agitated, and finally a medley of yelps being emitted as she relived the excitement of the day.

My first excursions with gun and dog were into the Spring Coppice after roosting pigeons. At first I could just make it to a spot near a huge oak tree known as 'King Oak', towering above its fellows in a wonderful stand of mature timber. In the Spring of the year pigeons were all feeding out in the fields. A few minutes sufficed to make a screen to hide behind, an armful of dead bracken would be collected and laced into a nearby bush. Simple but effective. Then we would await the woodies coming in to roost.

Those evenings stand out as some of the most pleasant in a lifetime of shooting. Given a strong wind, pigeons coming to roost in high timber can give the most exacting and difficult shots anyone could possibly wish for. In practice the ratio of cartridges expended to the number of kills is amazingly high. Indeed compared with any other class of game I am sure it is quite the highest. By no means are all evenings ideal for the sport, but even so what an immense amount of satisfaction can be derived from sharing that woodland solitude with your dog, eyes scanning through and beyond the nearby tree tops to spot the incoming woodies. How often deceived by the flight of a bird as small as a chaffinch or a tomtit flitting to another twig.

As time passes your disturbing presence is to some extent accepted and activity is gradually resumed all around. There is never a single dull moment: the bird-song is continuous, some distance away a pair of courting pigeons are amusing, the occasional flight of the cock, dipping then rising again and at its peak those resounding wing-claps, loud and strong. Yet resentment can still be heard, expressed by a pair of magpies, audible from point to point, but never seen. A peggy whitethroat with nest in a nearby break of brambles is angry and scolds. Not so the monotonous chiff-chaff or a chaffinch with that oft repeated ditty, not unlike the yellow-hammer's hedgerow song.

A grunt from the spaniel and looking away through the tree tops into the distance – no mistake this time – the first of the woodies are coming in. At the very last moment they swing wide and settle in the top branches of King Oak. There is the beat of powerful wings as unseen swans follow the course of the river down the valley.

Suddenly one feels a silence, a complete hush, even the twitterings cease as a sparrowhawk glides to a dead branch, stretches each wing in turn then begins to preen himself. Much too early for him to think of retiring and he may well have another kill and meal before doing so. He is one of the very last to seek his roost. Once in Morrell's Coppice, late in the dusk a sparrow-hawk glided in and settled on a branch of the tree I was standing beneath. As I looked up he dropped his kill in fright and a lesser spotted woodpecker fell at my feet.

An evening spent this way is so much more rewarding

than any amount of walking through a wood. It is so typical of the opportunities I have enjoyed throughout a lifetime spent getting to know a little of the creatures of wood, stream and field. The absolute peace of it all in those distant days broken only by the puffing of a friendly train across the valley, its sound soon dying away. A faint whistle, perhaps as far away as Ironbridge and once again all is quiet.

Tap, tap, tap from a nearby tree, just a great tit in quest of food, but the wonder is how small a bird can strike so hard to make such a noise. A tree-creeper, how rightly named, firmly believes in starting at the bottom, invariably alighting on the butt of a tree and working his way upwards. His erratic zig-zag movements are mouse-like, at times lost to sight as he rounds the trunk, but quickly back in view again and always working upwards. None too thorough in his search, he will soon leave that tree, but within a short space of time will return to it. Glimpse of a nuthatch, gulls high overhead and beyond the Severn the curlew's unforgettable Spring song.

As evening closes in pigeons will leave the high timber and drop into the conifers further down the bank. Much later those chuckling elusive magpies will go to roost tucked close in to the bole of a larch and jays too will pass the night in similar fashion. And right into the dusk, carrion crows will pass over in twos and threes. They too have their favourite roost in a wood across the river. Clumps of laurel and box will afford shelter to the tit family and a host of other small birds.

You know a pigeon makes wonderfully good eating: why they are not more popular I just do not know. My mother cooked them in different ways, often in pies, sometimes parboiled and then roasted. My favourite was when she did them in one of the old-fashioned brown stewpots, cooked slowly with vegetables for a very long time, the whole delicious dish topped by a suet crust – a good thick one about an inch thick!

◇◇◇◇◇◇◇◇◇

16

CONEY RECOLLECTIONS

A feature of the Spring Coppice shoots in the late 1800s was the huge number of rabbits killed. For several days preceding these shoots rabbits were 'stunk' from their burrows and the holes filled in. Unbelievable as it now seems they were also netted from outlying parts of the estate and turned down for the shooting. Of course this was before my time, but recounted by the old hands, they with memories of the paunching and hanging of vast numbers until two o'clock in the morning. Bags of more than a thousand are recorded in the game book.

When we arrived at Apley, rabbits were so numerous that fields running away from the house and bordering the Spring Coppice simply appeared to be moving of an evening. On coming to the estate, my father's instructions had been to reduce their numbers to the lowest possible level. As the years went by they were in fact got down to a reasonable level. Then came the Great War, and with control measures having to be largely abandoned, rabbit numbers increased again at an alarming rate.

As keepers returned to normal duties after the war, great efforts were made to reduce their numbers once more. Snaring, ferreting, long-netting, trapping and shooting all were employed Gassing of course was not an option at that time. These activities continued from October through to the following March. In the park it was possible to set three hundred snares at a time on four different sites before the whole area was covered. Catches varied, weather usually being the deciding factor. A dry night with a good strong wind was ideal.

One lovely night in late October we had a great catch. Snares were always visited in the early night and rabbits removed. George, the lad here at the time, was with me and we had just started the round when a figure loomed up. It was the Stockton End beat keeper, complete with game bag, who jokingly said, 'I can carry all you can catch.' No idle boast as there was six foot of him all brawn and muscle. First we filled his game bag, then the game pockets inside his jacket, and finally traced them in strings over his shoulders

It was the beginning of the rut of the Fallow deer. The bucks had a habit of scraping out holes, often feet deep and three or four feet wide, which they wallowed in. The one in question was beneath a large beech tree and into it plopped Jim. There he stayed completely helpless, totally immobilised by the weight of rabbit. In the morning snares were looked at again; that particular catch was one of the best we ever had, one hundred and four rabbits!

Four or five rabbits to a score of snares was satisfactory. Results were often disappointing, snares being knocked over by cattle, deer or sheep, the latter being the greater nuisance. A knot was tied in each snare to prevent the open noose from closing completely and thereby allowing a sheep or deer to free themselves. Quiet, misty, muggy weather produced the worst conditions. If the later part of the night got out fine following rain that could give good results. Foxes were troublesome, often spoiling many rabbits.

Over one period of several months Jim White and I averaged thirty-three daily when ferreting. I shot with a sixteen bore made by Pape of Newcastle, a delightful weapon and greatly prized. Bolted rabbits gave excellent sport and on rough or broken ground provided the most exacting of shots. My ambition was twenty consecutive kills, but I never managed to achieve it, though reaching sixteen on several occasions. How often bunny jinked just as that trigger was squeezed!

We were never very successful at long-netting but it had a fascination all of its own. In this particular branch the laddies from Ironbridge were miles ahead of us, doubtless emphasising that old saying – practice makes perfect. They certainly had not only the practice but also the incentive, for to a great extent their main source of income was dependent on the success of their nightly forays.

One evening I accompanied a friend who had visited us from the west side of the river and bade him goodnight at Trottie's grave. Trottie was a horse which lived to the considerable age of thirty two and the children of W. H Foster had all learned to ride on her. Returning home along a narrow woodland tract, a figure loomed up in front of me. I stepped off the path and he and four others trudged past, nearly touching me, all in complete silence. I hurried home and my father and I spent the rest of the night looking for them. Their original plans would almost certainly have been changed by our meeting. Many times since I have wondered just where their activities did begin on that particular evening.

Perhaps I should explain that on their long-netting forays those men always carried sticks, probably staffs would be a better description, for they were upwards of five feet long and one and a half inches in diameter. When driving rabbits from their feeding ground towards the long-net the staffs were used to thump the ground. Completely silent, it was a highly effective way of starting the conies into full flight for home. Again when transporting their catch a goodly number of rabbits, legged and coupled in pairs, could be slung on a staff carried over the shoulder.

Of course they did have yet another use and that was not an aid to walking. It could well explain though the leather and wicker-work shields which used to hang in the attics at Apley Lodge!

Apart from gain, admittedly the driving force, something else in their make-up contributed to their way of life. Excitement and risks taken, maybe the sheer joy and satisfaction of wrong-doing, who knows? Whatever the driving force those nightly excursions were not carried out by lazy men for they operated over a wide area, often walking many miles to distant venues. After a successful foray there was the haul of conies to be carried and I know from experience just how tiring that can be. Nets and pegs all added to the load. They also had to make their way home unobserved. Sometimes the catch was hidden and collected later by horse and trap.

One night a bobby apprehended two of the laddies complete with netting gear and a number of rabbits. Refusing to carry the latter they dumped them on the ground so the P.C. picked them up and carried them himself. A mile or so further on they thanked him saying they were nearly home, could manage the rest of the way and would relieve him of the load. At the same time they produced a piece of paper signed by a local farmer stating they had permission to catch rabbits on his land!

Their visits to any one place were infrequent, probably only once or twice a year. Those occasions invariably coincided with a marked reduction in the numbers of rabbits living there.

◇◇◇◇◇◇◇◇◇

17

ONE WILD NIGHT

One wild night during the 1920s brings back vivid recollections. It began with an exceptionally bad gale, a sky of low storm-tossed cloud flicking by on a November day. Rising and falling in fitful gusts, the wind scattered showers of golden russet leaves through the air. Others were sent cartwheeling and gambolling across the fields, some checked by tufts of grass and hollows in the ground – only to be gyrated on again by a following stronger gust, finally to be embedded in the fence row on the far side of the field. Next morning they were feet deep, probably giving extra protection to a hibernating hedgehog in its nest in the heart of the fence.

Great flocks of plover against the horizon, wheeling, rising then dropping in the sky. Wood pigeons ceaselessly in flight. Fieldfare and starling, small bunches of linnets and other seed-eating birds. All supremely restless and disturbed. As the afternoon wore on those early fitful gusts gave place to a roar that rose and fell, the wind swaying the pines and larch, now and again relenting and easing off as a cat might play with a bird or mouse.

Small branches were even then being snapped off and rotten branches brought crashing down bringing fear and terror to the denizens within. I watched hares with lugs flattened to their heads leaving the woods for the open fields and as the dusk approached rabbits followed in their wake. Stranger still, pheasants quitted the wood and made for the open fence rows.

As night closed in, the storm increased in violence and its anger no longer spared the trees or the lives of the creatures within. By morning practically the whole of Morrells Coppice was a complete shambles, presenting a scene of disorder and destruction sad to see.

During the previous evening I had left my house and had struggled against the fury of the storm down an old lane and in doing so disturbed a pheasant which rose into the wind, then flung back over my head like a bullet. Death surely ended that last mad flight. Nature can be both kind and cruel!

Bob: the Time Machine – 'in a class of his own'.

◇◇◇◇◇◇◇◇◇

18

DOG WATCH

My spaniel Jess had a litter of nine pups. Quite amazingly all nine were male, each one beautifully marked with that distinctive patch of tan above the eye. Two of them, Bob and Roy, went to my brother in Norfolk and we were able to follow their lives. Bob (pictured opposite) was a great character and a most outstanding worker. Ted and Kit told us that every morning, dead on six o'clock, Bob came to their bedroom from the kitchen where he slept. Later we were staying with them and sure enough, dead on the stroke of six each morning, Bob could be heard plonking up the stairs!

Just how he did this was a complete and utter mystery. Chiming clocks were stopped and clock faces turned to walls. Every possible noise which could possibly have acted as a timepiece either inside the house or outdoors was checked. It was thought their move to the Via Gellia in Derbyshire might upset him. But no! Bob arrived upstairs bang on time. The mystery remained unsolved right to the very end!

One other side to this tale. Nothing, literally nothing, could induce Robert to leave his bed one moment before 6am! Spaniels are noted individualists and he was in a class of his very own.

19

◇◇◇◇◇◇◇◇◇

SNOW IN NORFOLK

One November in the early 1920s I spent a few days with my brother who at that time was a Head Keeper in Norfolk. Ted was waiting when we pulled into Melton Constable station some time after dark. Great heaps of snow were piled high on the platform. He said 'I'm sorry but you will have to walk. I started out with the pony and trap but stuck in a drift and have had to leave the pony at a farm nearby.' So, complete with Gladstone bag, we started on our three-mile walk. Time and again snow drifting in a bitterly cold wind made it necessary to leave the road and walk in the fields. There were numerous flashes of lightning and accompanying peals of thunder. The former revealed massive black snow clouds and illuminated that flat countryside, that vast expanse of whiteness and its stark leafless trees with a bluish and somewhat eerie light. A night to remember and the only time I can ever recall such a combination, snow, thunder and lightning.

It was all so worthwhile for a wonderful welcome from my sister-in-law Kit and the spaniels, Bob and Roy, was followed by a delicious hot meal. So very welcome and how kept in such perfect condition something of a culinary mystery for we were mighty late getting in.

A shoot had been arranged for the day following that wild night and despite such adverse conditions was thoroughly enjoyed. A great many birds fell into deep snow and could only

*A Norfolk Shoot in the 1920s. The shooting brake was elegant but
hardly designed for cross-country work.*

be spotted by their tail tips sticking out of it. Next day we found
that the Corby crows were infinitely more adept than we were at
finding any which had not been picked up.

As invariably happens following a heavy snow, severe frost
sct in giving most wonderful nights of brilliant moonlight. From
the coast a mighty cannonade of fowling pieces could be heard
booming and rattling away. In the local of an evening there was a
throng of Norfolk countrymen, many of the older ones sporting
spade beards, a buzz of Norfolk dialect and the ritual heating of
pokers in a roaring fire to be followed by the supping of mulled
ale. Pleasant memories of my one-and-only visit to that beautiful
county of abundant game and big skies.

20

GOLDEN YEARS

In 1924 the death of the old squire was followed by my father's retirement only a few years later. Between them they had more than upheld and consolidated the sporting traditions which had so long been a feature of the Apley Estate. In 1928 I took my father's place as Head Keeper and was married that December. On the evening of our return from honeymoon in London a message awaited me to get game the following day. We met at Higford and walked a field of frozen sugar beet in a strong and searching wind. I was home again in time for lunch having shot twenty three pheasants and thankful to get out of that bitter wind on an intensely cold day.

The Major was practical and never wasted words. Many times I left his study when little appeared to have been said, but on subsequent reflection realised I had come into the devil of a lot of work. Following his succession the number and range of guests visiting Apley increased. Looking back through the records what an impressive crowd they were. Many of the leading titles in the land, a sprinkling of diplomats and politicians, Royalty on a few occasions, HRH The Duke of Kent taking part in the shooting.

From year to year, shooting parties tended to follow a pattern, each one built around three or four 'regulars'. For instance one of them always consisted of Blues officers either serving or retired. Most summers the Major spent several months in Austria

*Norman and Minnie Sharpe, 1936. Spaniels were still in vogue
but labs were replacing the curlies*

and each season a party of Austrian counts and princes shot at
Apley. Completely sincere, never ostentatious, he was a wonderful
host, the shooting a means of entertaining his friends. Emphasis
was on quality and standards were of the highest This period of
years up to the second World War, I have heard referred to as 'The
Golden years of Apley'.

Certainly they were full of interest and hard work.
Additional staff was engaged and every aspect of the game management was intensified. Pheasants were reared on all the beats except
the one over the river and partridge driving was reintroduced. A
few of the old hands could remember them being driven when
Captain James Foster had run the shooting for a few years. As
near as I could ascertain this occurred during the 1890s, successful

days and good bags being recorded. Following that brief spell of driving, walking up was resumed and continued right up to the period I am describing.

Two new shooting stands were cut out in The Terrace and two more in the Spring Coppice. An indoor sitting house was built with capacity to accommodate nearly four hundred broodies. New laying pens were erected and additional eggs were purchased from the game farms.

In November 1929 the Long Pool was stocked with rainbow trout. Most days I threw in a few handfuls of biscuit meal and was concerned by the lack of activity. Apart from the occasional rise there was no sign of them. One stormy evening the following March I took a fly rod down and quickly satisfied myself all was well. Nearly every cast brought a fish and in a few brief minutes I had caught and returned several in A1 condition. For the following year or two the pool was restocked but then Canadian pond weed appeared and in a short time the water was choked by it. Everything was tried, cutting with chain saws, a flat bottomed punt equipped with a knife sweeping before it, even scythes and brushing hooks but after all this the weed won and

Sitting hens being fed – the indoor sitting house is in the background

*Wattle hurdles were erected and lined with brash to provide shelter for
laying birds. The eggs were collected daily.*

completely choked the pool for several years. After that it lost its
initial vitality and gradually faded away. Today it is still there but
with a retarded growth of only a few inches.

From the early 1930s three hundred mallard were reared.
These were eventually released on the Long Pool where hand-
feeding continued until they were shot. Usually they provided
good sport for a couple of evenings after which they dispersed
and could look after themselves very well indeed. Many moved
to the Severn but some settled on the pools in the park. When a
few hours sport were required at short notice for a guest or two
staying at the Hall these could prove more than useful. On one of
these occasions duck were driven off a small pool and went away
in string formation high over a waiting gun. A shot was fired and
the tail bird crumpled out of the air beautifully shot. Someone
remarked what a good shot. 'Yes,' replied the gun, 'Wasn't it, but
what an unlucky bird. I shot at the leading one!'

In 1937 the head river keeper of the Houghton Club at
Stockbridge was engaged to advise on improving the fishing
potential of the Worfe. First he did a survey of the possibilities of
Allscott pools as a trout hatchery. This he advised against. Next

day Major Foster, Sir John Milbanke, Mr Roney-Dougal the agent and myself spent a most interesting day with Alf Lunn who made an inspection of the river itself. His report suggested the stream be netted again to remove coarse fish. Water pH was satisfactory though slightly acid and river fauna fairly good. There was a lack of suitable weed and some suggestions were made regarding control of the flow to create better holding pools.

As a result of his visit it was decided to engage a man as river keeper, to create two spawning beds and to introduce fly boards to the water. These were eight feet long, some eight inches wide and attached at one end to a length of wire which allowed the board to rise and fall as the river varied in height. A post driven into the bed of the stream acted as anchor. When ready to lay their eggs some species of water fly drift down with the current until they hit an obstruction. They then crawl beneath to deposit their eggs. After a few days the underside of the board is coated with dabs of spawn-like substance which in the course of time break up to release the minute eggs which drift away into the silt and weed beds, a renewal of life. Once 'filled' these boards can be moved to areas deficient in fly life.

On a later date I went to Stockbridge and a visit to the Berkshire Fishery at Hungerford was arranged for us to purchase 250 twelve-inch trout and fifty larger fish of at least one and a half pounds. A further visit was made to Stockbridge in early November. The day was fine and sunny and I was given a demonstration of pike snaring. With its bed of chalk, the Test was crystal clear. Given favourable light conditions, objects were easily visible at considerable depths. I was told to look for a pike's head protruding from a weed bed. One was soon spotted. A long bamboo pole with an ordinary rabbit snare fixed to its end was gently lowered well above the fish and guided downstream to the middle of its body. Then a quick snatch and haul in, hand over hand.

A second was caught. The third was alarmed by a clumsy approach and dashed away. Alf said 'Watch for a cloud of chalk where he settles', and sure enough this swirl of white showed a little distance upstream. He was quickly located again and this time there was no mistake. Several big grayling could be seen lying on the bottom in really deep water. Alf cleverly snared one. It all looked so easy!

That afternoon I fished for grayling. Alf Lunn told me to work downstream and he would join me at The Sheepwash. This I did with little success until he joined me. After that the fun really started and I caught a bass carrier bag full which I brought home the following day.

Weed was brought from Stockbridge and a nursery of it established. Ranunculus, water celery, milfoil and starwort all thrived and were transplanted to selected reaches of the river. Additional areas of good fishing water were created by using large piles to increase the rate of flow. Excellent fishing was enjoyed the following season and a number of the larger fish were taken. Like so many other things, this interesting experiment came to an abrupt end with the war.

Netting the Worfe. The river level was lowered to facilitate this exercise.

Fortunately the woods at Apley were perfectly situated to give wonderful shooting which tested the best. The Terrace shoot is outstanding, its steep slopes and jutting outcrops ideal for presenting high, fast flying birds and all in a setting of great beauty. How often have I seen first class shots completely fail to deal with them. Known as The Horseshoe, the first stand can be spectacular. Birds are flushed off a circular projection of the wood with the guns standing in a half moon formation in parkland below. With a breeze blowing and a dry sharp atmosphere they provide wonderful shooting. Few fly straight but curl away to the flanks and so many are in that deceptive downward glide, probably the most difficult shot of all. My diary records one extremely crisp and windy day when birds flew like the very devil and a first class team of guns fired over one thousand shots there for just one hundred and forty birds! Believe me I have seen some mighty long faces after the Horseshoe drive, some famous shooting names amongst them!

I was very fond of the Bromley day with its hillsides rising steeply from the Severn and Worfe. Its woods were superbly placed but so much smaller and more easily controlled. The Spring Coppice shoot took in two miles of wooded hillside, again climbing away from the Severn and also some of the outlying parkland plantations.

Patmarsh beat was quite different in character. Most of its woods nestle in depressions. To give the best shooting, maximum use had to be made of cover crops growing in surrounding fields overlooking the woodland. Wild pheasants always contributed heavily to the bag at Patmarsh and it was invariably a most pleasant day.

When speaking of Patmarsh, a couple of incidents always spring to mind. A grand little spinney called Bailey's Corner lies a field's breadth away from the main Patmarsh wood and was being driven out towards it. This was always a natural flight. Throughout the previous night a gale had raged and the morning was still stormy. Practically every bird in that drive flew straight back over the beaters' heads and settled again behind them. Many times since I have pondered over this and am certain their behaviour on that occasion was entirely due to the buffeting of the previous night.

The other incident. Many years ago I was loading for Mr Guy Fenwick when a close packed covey of partridges lifted over the fence. The gun took the leading bird and five came tippling down!

But to return to the shooting. The record bag was made in The Terrace by a team comprising the Earls of Dudley and Pembroke, Messrs Cobbold and Somerset, the Marquis of Anglesey and Major Foster. A wonderful opening stand of 334 at The Horseshoe set the tone for the day which finished with a total of 953. It was one of those days when, apart from the last drive, everything went right. A couple of foxes got into the heading corner and caused an almighty flush. The air was full of birds and an excellent drive was ruined. A great number of pheasants were necessary to kill a good bag in The Terrace. Each drive was dependent on fresh birds as few were ever shown from the preceding ones.

Lunch break outside the Harness Room at Apley Lodge in the 1930s

◇◇◇◇◇◇◇◇◇

21

CONIES AND CRUFTS

Life was full, so full indeed it was never easy to get away for a few days. There were however two 'musts' in the calendar. Crufts dog show was one of them and almost invariably we managed to spend a few days with brother Ted and his wife Kit in the Via Gellia valley. There was always a couple of days ferreting on those steep hillsides and great fun it was. Clumps of elder were much favoured by the bunnies. On that rocky terrain burrows were shallow and with a few ferrets quietly dropped into the holes, the conies bolted well. They gave most excellent sport, snap shooting at its very best!

It may have been something of a busman's holiday but after the end of the shooting season that annual visit to Crufts dog show was the event of the year for many Head Keepers. It was a tradition which had been established by my father's generation in the early days of the show. Rapidly it became a focal point where these men could meet, compare notes, renew friendships, generally keep abreast of developments and have a rattling good time whilst doing so!

After one of those visits my father arrived home the proud owner of a Bedlington terrier. This to my mother's intense annoyance! She need not have worried. Father had the Bedlington on a lead and on being released he showed his appreciation by chasing and killing three or four hens in less time than it takes to describe. An altogether exhilarating beginning, and end, to his stay at Apley Lodge!

An unusual London sight occurred in the early days when my Uncle Isaac, Tommy Tullet senior and Davie Miller hailed a hansom cab. Somehow or other, Lord only knows how, the three of them managed to scramble in and the floor fell clean out of the cab. Hardly surprising. They were not built to take sixty odd stone!

On entering the show, noise was perhaps the first impression. A mighty chorus of sound, yippy, staccato yaps from the little fellows ranging down the scale to the baying of the big boys. Dogs of every description. Long rows of benches were partitioned off into individual bays. A walk through those lines was usually the first activity and certainly rewarding. Specimens all, the cream of the doggy world. I can visualise them now. Speak of character in the human race? They had all the expressions: self pity, friendliness, keep your distance, bored stiff, only one day more. Lets be fair, so many, especially the little chaps asking only for a friendly word and pat on the head.

The Likely Lads again – thirty years on. Brother Ted in the side-car.

For fieldsports the pre-1914 era represented a pinnacle which has never been surpassed and the links forged with Crufts at that time were due, not only to the popularity of the sporting dog, but also its importance to the commercial side. Every manufacturer of game and dog food or appliances appeared to have a stand. All the game farms were there, also the gunsmiths and clothiers. It seemed they vied with each other in dispensing hospitality. Refreshments were ad lib and their consumption great. Amusing to wander round the stands and listen to the buzz of conversation. With keepers assessing and discussing the products on display it was truly representative of the brogues and dialects of the British Isles.

Right up until the second World War the main emphasis was still on the sporting dog. Practically the whole of the ground floor was given over to them. Classes were huge and judging decisions must indeed have been difficult with quality of the entrants so uniformly high. All the emotions of the human character were to be seen whilst watching a class being judged. Intense concentration from both judges and handlers. Elation and dejection, perhaps that agonising mute appeal to the judges greatest of them all. Ringside spectators, many with a personal interest in what was happening at the centre of the ring, could reveal dismay, disbelief and also joy, but throughout it all there was an intensity one could really feel. So many of those spectators were really knowledgeable. Each breed of dog had its own crowd of supporters many of whom were keepers.

Altogether it was a unique get-together of the sporting world, the link with the big estates where vast numbers of game were reared and large staffs employed always so evident. On one occasion brother Ted produced one of the old Knowsley record cards which I still retain. It was for 1913 and the total for that season was 16,647 head. A sub-heading stated that out of that total cock shooting and other small days accounted for 4,858 pheasants, 264 partridges, 1,119 hares, 56 rabbits, 67 woodcock, 17 snipe and 500 duck. When my brother joined the staff under Alex McLauchlan there were 32 beat keepers each rearing a hundred coops.

In passing it is fair to say that as a shot Ted had few equals. His speed was quite remarkable as was his power of observation, and because of his deadly accuracy he shot on most of the bye days mentioned. In addition he was, and in fact still is, a most amazing rifle shot.

Another memory of Crufts also lingers. I still recall coming out of the show onto those rather dreary streets, always cold, sometimes with snow showers, and in them the ill clad, undernourished ex-soldiers playing music for what they could collect. A stark, haunting contrast from the world of Crufts and I counted myself fortunate indeed!

KNOWSLEY.

DATE. 1913.	BEATS.	No. Guns.	Pheasants.	Partridges.	Hares.	Rabbits.	Woodcocks.	Snipe.	Ducks	TOTAL.
Oct. 7	Roby Carrs ...	3	47	20	64	2	...	...	...	133
,, 18	King's Moss ...	6	80	41	187	8	1	...	9	326
,, 20	Scarth Hill	5	60	13	313	1	...	...	...	387
Nov. 10	Huyton and Roby	6	66	15	143	...	...	...	...	224
,, 18	Bickerstaffe ...	8	584	4	356	5	1	...	2	952
,, 19	Stockbridge... ...	7	495	14	260	3	1	...	...	773
,, 20	Emma Wood ...	7	834	10	201	19	1	3	...	1068
,, 21	Knowsley	6	516	9	208	4	...	1	3	741
Dec. 9	Park	8	1564	2	6	10	10	1	1	1594
,, 10	Mossboro'	7	969	22	224	22	4	...	11	1252
,, 12	Meadows	8	1474	6	70	2	2	...	...	1554
,, 27	Nursery	6	209	4	166	3	...	1	33	416
,, 30	Simonswood ...	6	193	4	296	16	5	...	...	514
	Cock Shooting & other small days	...	4858	100	1119	58	67	11	500	6713
	TOTALS		11949	264	3613	153	92	17	559	16647

Knowsley Game Card

22

◇◇◇◇◇◇◇◇◇

MY FAVOURITE BIRD

It was possible to shoot on the partridge beats for six separate days without covering any of the ground previously shot over. These days were invariably organised to employ two sets of beaters. The Euston System was used and a brief description of the method is justified as in practice it was most interesting.

Every possible nest was searched for and recorded. From these nests, eggs were collected daily as they were laid. As each egg was removed it was replaced by a dummy until the partridge had finished laying her clutch and settled down to sit on a clutch of dummies. Eggs which had been collected were set under bantams in batches of about two hundred. Using this system some eggs were being incubated as others continued to be laid.

One great objective was to reduce the period of brooding and in so doing lessen the many and varied hazards faced by a sitting partridge. Another was to extend the hatching period, thereby ensuring at least some good weather during the actual hatching off.

From about the twelfth day it was safe to replace the dummies with clutches of chipped eggs incubated by the bantams and in so doing reduce the natural sitting period by half. The nest was approached very quietly and the bird gently eased off. Usually she just slid away into thick herbage and a clutch of warm eggs was quickly placed in the nest before making a hasty retreat. A few hours later the site was revisited to check that all was well.

Few partridges nest before the first week in May. Hedgerows provide the favourite cover and their choice of a site is both painstaking and time-consuming. Often several nests are fashioned but left unlined until a final choice is made. From the first egg being laid they are completely concealed between visits by a covering of dead leaves and herbage some half inch deep. Within three days of the final egg being laid, this covering is dispensed with, leaving the eggs fully exposed until the hen finally goes down to sit.

This offers a great opportunity to that master thief of all, the magpie. Jays, rooks and jackdaws are just as fond of a tasty meal of eggs and there are other contenders, notably the carrion crow. An even greater risk phase is the final two or three days before the chicks actually hatch. A restlessness develops which is marked by fluffing out of feathers so that scent of the hen is more widely and strongly diffused. How often a victim in those last few crucial hours falls to either fox or cat and there are many others. Nature behaves in curious ways and often appears to have a leaning towards the rag, tag and bobtail or perhaps an even better definition, the underworld members of society.

Perhaps the greatest claim for the Euston system was the constant supervision involving daily inspection of nests. So often clutches of eggs can be saved Causes of loss can be surprising and unexpected to say the very least. Eggs displaced by a mole burrowing under the nest, a farm implement thrown into the fence, are but two of what can be called accidental mishaps. Over a season the percentage can be quite amazingly high.

With the Euston system, a final residue of eggs was usually hatched out under bantams. From season to season numbers varied in relation to losses during the previous weeks. Sometimes there was only the odd coop or two. One season Jim Pryke successfully reared towards two hundred by the open range method.

In course of time these were taken to the fields. Coops were staggered over a large acreage and placed a considerable distance from one another. Despite this they had packed together within a few weeks and frequently came back to visit the field where they had been reared.

From a shooting point of view they were a failure. They rose in a cloud and flew straight back over the beaters' heads to where they had been reared. A few years later Pollard reared another batch of about a hundred on the same beat. This time they were in a large field of roots which was being driven and the day was a very wet one. For the drive in question the guns stood behind a high fence and this time the hand-reared birds did provide quite a lot of shooting, but they were difficult to get up and many failed to rise until the final few yards of the field were beaten out. It was altogether unsatisfactory as so many were not worth shooting.

No doubt the adverse weather conditions were partly responsible but the contrast with the wild coveys which flew well was remarkable. When reared artificially they tend to become very tame and probably this has much to do with their unnatural behaviour on release to the wild. Yet what delightful little fellows they are to rear. Their dance on a coop lid when being fed with ant eggs was a most pleasing and amusing sight. A healthy sprinkling of ants always arrived with the eggs and the dance prevented them climbing up their legs. Ant eggs would be nearly impossible to obtain in quantity nowadays. They, like so many other insects, have hit hard times. At Patmarsh one hot September day, a hand reared covey clucked their way into and through the house and around the legs of the shooting party lunching there.

To bring a good day's partridge shooting using two sets of drivers to a successful conclusion has, I believe, given me more satisfaction than if I had actually been shooting. And I have taken part in many such shoots. So much has gone into the preparation for such a day. A constant picture of the ground to be covered, the quantity and habits of the birds on it, their natural lines of flight and feeding routine must all be borne in mind.

With the ever-changing pattern of cropping each season brings its own challenge. New plans are called for with holding crops of cover being the dominant factor. No final decision can be taken until a day or two before the shoot, as farm work is changing the landscape daily. Every detail must be thrashed out with the beat keepers, timing and transport and possible alterations which could arise during the day. To mention but one, the possibility of gales or strong wind had always to be taken into account. Stands were pegged out, fences screened for the guns where necessary and brashed hurdles erected for them to stand behind on open ground.

A good start to the day is worth a deal. It must mean a lot to any host and the most hardened and experienced head or beat keeper is by no means immune to a certain sense of relief. Not all days begin well and I recall one in particular. It was 1935, a marvellous partridge year. Harrington, New House and Norton farms were to be shot over and there was a wonderful head of game. An evening or two previously Griffin and I had walked a stubble and the fact we had put off fourteen coveys all into their teens gave expectations of a wonderful start to the day ahead.

The guns were Maj. Gen. Sir R. Howard-Vyse, Sir R. Molyneaux, Lord Ilchester, Gen. Sir C. Grant, The Hon. E.S. Wyndham, Sir Tom Lea and the Major. A good team. It was a foggy morning and vegetation was beaded with moisture. The first drive out of roots was a complete blank and there was a depression one could feel. At the second drive, again out of roots, one shot was fired at the only bird in it, a red-leg. It seemed impossible.

By this time the Major was somewhat red in the face and with good reason. He asked me what had gone wrong and I said I just did not know. Drive number three was from Harrington

House out of a field called Cabbage Corner. It was simply full of birds, covey upon covey going forward over the guns. Only on one other occasion have I seen more birds in a field and that was at Bromley. Radiant faces dispelled the gloom, perhaps all but those of mine and Griffin, for we knew just how outstanding it could have been if the first two drives had been successful. They had been planned to feed Cabbage Corner which was to have been the return drive with broken up coveys from the first two. It could have been memorable!

Later I learned exactly what had happened. A few men detailed to drive open ground into the two fields of roots had arrived just in time to see a party of mushroomers leaving in the opposite direction and lifting covey after covey into Cabbage Corner. That afternoon 95 brace were shot on Norton Farm making the day's bag 150 brace. On the previous day 139½ brace had been shot on the Patmarsh beat by much the same team. .

Another shoot at Bromley that same year I recall with very mixed feelings. It could, indeed it should, have been a record day. As it was, we killed just 117 brace. With only average shooting it would have topped the three hundred mark. As it was the marksmanship was quite unbelievably poor. Next morning I was at Apley and the Major remarked, 'It was a good day yesterday.' I replied, 'Yes, but most disappointing.' He knew exactly what I had in mind and said, 'The number of the bag doesn't interest me.'

To a great extent he was right for even in those days I was beginning to tire of the numbers game. As host and Head Keeper we both aimed at providing the highest possible quality of shooting, and sporting standards were never sacrificed for records at Apley. Just prior to this particular shoot though the Himley, people had shot 250 brace and were somewhat cock-a-hoop about it. Human nature being what it is I must confess I would so dearly love to have pipped them!

That day at Bromley probably illustrates to perfection a factor which can so easily be overlooked when going through game records. In fact the Apley records hardly reflect the wonderful head of game, partridges in particular, which the estate carried during the late Twenties and Thirties. Probably a far more realistic picture emerges when we look at the bye-days. Those were often for the pot and were both carefree and enjoyable.

It was 1934 when my brother helped me to shoot cock pheasants. On three consecutive days we topped 150! Another day stands out. The Major, Sir John Milbanke, Tom Grey and myself were shooting and we had two drives from the Leavenhalls and Ewdness ground over the main road. Sir John went lame and he and the Major went home. There had been a great many birds in those two drives and we were told to carry on and shoot all we could. A large field of sugar beet was walked and we shot 30 brace within the hour. On another day that season my brother and I shot 51 brace of partridges on the Newton farm.

Field Trial, 1928. Norman, extreme right, at the head of his flock.

Before leaving the partridge a brief look, not only at the effect adverse weather can have, but also the quite staggering resilience of this my favourite bird. In 1928, Retriever Trials were held on the estate. Lorna, Countess Howe, Sir W. Bromley-Davenport and Col. Wilson were judging. Of the total of 149 head of game shot in two consecutive days there were no fewer than 47 partridges. I mention this as only 269 were shot in that whole season which must rank with the very worst. Next year 629 were shot and by 1930, just two short years later, the total was just under the thousand!

23

THE POINTING DOG

My Uncle Isaac of Keith died in 1938. Apart from the personal sense of loss the event somehow seemed symbolic. Here was a man who had lived at the very heart of the gun and dog world throughout its two greatest eras. World War I brought an end to the first of these and it had become ominously clear that the second was destined to share the same fate in the all-too-immediate future. Time had run out for Isaac but how much he had crowded into a lifetime.

For Isaac the die was cast at an early age. I have heard my father say their parents used to pay sixpence (2½p) a week to send them to school. One day Grandfather went to pay the school master who said 'This is too much.' 'Well' said Grandfather 'There's Ted, Tom, Isaac and...' 'Stop' interrupted the school master, 'We haven't seen Isaac for the last six weeks!' It was true. He had played truant for all that time. Not a bad record, but next day he joined my father as an under keeper on the Ravensworth estate.

At that time the new Head Keeper there was also something of a character. It was a notorious district for poaching and one day two of the laddies were busy rabbiting when the man himself rode into the field on horseback with a shotgun slung across his back. Spotting them he galloped across and reined in some distance away. 'Get going', said one. 'I know him. He'll shoot!' 'Never

'Stylish' Springers at Douglas Brae. They were descendants of Stylish Nellie, winner of the first ever Spaniel Field Trail organised by William Artwright in 1899.

man, never. Not him,' said the other as they grabbed their gear. Then, 'By God he will though,' as two charges of shot whistled around them.

Leaving Ravensworth, Isaac went as Head Keeper to the Clayton family at The Chesters. It was an excellent position but the fascination of the working dog and lure of the Field Trial world proved too great. Within a few years he moved North to Keith and established his kennels. The Gordon setter held a particular fascination for him and he was largely responsible for re-establishing and bringing the breed back to prominence in this country.

At his death he was said to be the greatest gun dog authority of the century. This I quote from *Our Dogs* of 15th April 1938. To quote the paper again, 'Mr Sharpe owned the largest kennel of gun dogs in the world.' Undoubtedly he was one of the greatest authorities on the pointer and setter that ever lived. To begin to enumerate all his famous dogs is pointless. Truly the list was formidable and he achieved amazing success both in Field Trials and on the Bench. In 1901 he achieved a double feat winning the Kennel Club's field trial Derby with his Gordon setter, Stylish Ranger and championship of England with the gun.

Well after all that it will not surprise you that in the kennels at Douglas Brae, but a short distance from his home, some hundreds of dogs were housed, and exercised in a pen of several acres. Dogs were hired out for the Grouse season as most of the moors were still shot over them at that time. Each season the King took 35 at Balmoral. Whilst fishing at Ballindalloch this year the Head Keeper told me they had 14 of the dogs every year. Now I am told very few working pointers and setters remain in Scotland. Times change!

As a youngster I enjoyed some wonderful holidays at Keith. Invariably the day began early and if, as was often the case, just prior to the Grouse season, it was a matter of being on the

Stylish Sylph – one of Norman's favourite setters with which he won the Derby in 1913

moors at first light. Isaac, a handler or two and usually eight or ten pointers and setters. My job was invariably to hold three or four on leashes whilst others were put through their training. Believe me they could make the arms ache!

To watch them at work was fascination itself. Always in pairs they worked the area of moorland in front of the handler. Both dogs swept wide out to a flank, then back again crossing in front of him, and so on until one of them hit the wind of grouse. Immediately that beautiful rambling gallop stopped and the dog whipped round to point in the direction of the quarry. One front paw raised, tail out straight, an altogether pleasing sight. If properly trained, his partner reacted by stopping dead at once and lying down. After that the handler joined the pointing dog and quietly worked him up to the grouse. 'Ta-ho!' he said quietly and the dog moved forward a few paces before pointing again. 'Ta-ho!' again and so on until the birds were flushed at which point the dog instantly dropped flat to the ground.

This state of perfection was only attained by countless hours of training. As with all animal training it called for patience, great expertise and a quite surprising degree of physical endurance, qualities with which Isaac was well endowed. There can be few

A group of Stylish pointers – trained and hired out to the shooting estates for use of grouse moors when 'shooting over dogs' was the standard practice.

A Stylish pointer. With the demise of the pointer and the setter, sport has lost so much.

occupations which provide more frustration and exasperation, yet the reward lay in that state of perfection I have just described. A driven grouse or partridge may provide a better shot, but with the passing of the pointer and setter sport, has lost so much.

What a pleasure it has been to renew acquaintance with those sparkling Scottish streams in recent years. Seatrout and the odd salmon splashing heavily in the darkness as they obey nature's urge to reach the redds. Better still the thrill of a seatrout hooked in the dead of night, bats skimming the surface, an occasional moth fluttering into one, a branch of fishing unrivalled for sheer fascination and excitement.

By day when fishing for the silvery beauties, always the chance of spotting roe or red deer, golden monkey flowers and Scottish bluebell, goosanders winging up the river or shepherding their great broods of young on its boulder-strewn waters, oyster catchers, the odd capercaillie, all there to delight the eye still and so much more besides.

But how that countryside has changed since I was a lad. For one thing the rabbits are mightily reduced in numbers. For another so many sedgy acres have been brought into cultivation and that massive afforestation! Perhaps a deal to commend it but why carried out with such utter regimented disregard for the magnificent contours and variety of that glorious countryside and the wellbeing of the rivers it feeds?

24

WAR AGAIN

Storm clouds had gathered throughout the Thirties and in 1939 the inevitable happened. War once again with all its excitement, frustration, suffering and grief. Again it united the country in its supreme effort, perhaps as Churchill said, its finest hour.

Game was shot on the estate but the days of the large parties were over. Probably the best game years I can ever recall were those of the second war. They were quite exceptional partridge years. In 1939 we had a great many pheasants and the Major said we must shoot early to conserve food. That October we killed 531 in The Terrace before the leaf was off and undergrowth still dense. In November it was shot again and 664 were killed.

Two parallel paths ran though The Terrace. These were used by the walking guns who took birds going back or breaking out to the flanks. On this occasion I was instructed to take everything including birds going forward and shot 104 pheasants. By an amazing coincidence that was the only time I ever counted my bag but it is almost certain that is the most pheasants I ever shot in a day. That season I shot on no fewer than sixty days. Practically all the partridges were shot by walking up with the tenants joining in the shoots.

Apley Hall was turned into a Red Cross hospital for convalescent officers. There was a rapid build up of staff; an M.O., a colonel no less, a quarter master, matron, numerous sisters, nurses and orderlies. At last the great day came. The colonel donned his uniform and with matron and nursing staff in attendance awaited arrival of the first draft. It comprised one solitary officer who, it turned out, had been stung by a mosquito! He was there for a considerable time all on his own, poor chap. Later the hospital did fill up.

During those early war years the road to Apley Lodge was closed to traffic for a fortnight. A stick of bombs had landed in the area, three of them close to the road in question. There was some doubt whether they had exploded as they had thrown up cairns of soil but no crater. A week or two later the cairns caved in, one of them taking down a poor old cow which had to be destroyed. Those bombs fell just after dusk on a day when we had been shooting.

Frank Oakley had left his van at Apley Hall. He told me he had lost a wad of notes and was certain it was at the last stand. He had been standing by a small pond not far from the Hall. There was sufficient daylight left for me to go and look for the money whilst he went for his van. There it lay, a nice fat little wad, an elastic band holding it together! After that he joined us for tea before going home. Next morning revealed a new bomb crater; if not in the exact spot where the money had lain, then almighty close to it. War had not altered!

In passing a brief mention of 'Dad's Army'. In the beginning one might have been tempted to call it a ragtime force. It was never that. No force ever had more enthusiasm and determination. Oh dear me, it certainly had its comical side! Equipment and clothing arrived in driblets. On one occasion three pairs of gum boots, one pair retained in store, Joe Dyas another which did not fit and handed on to Albert Nichols, Fred Bott the remaining pair. A year or so later they were called in again. Albert, late of the 60th Rifles had made good use of his and they were about worn out. Fred, late of The Lancers, had his polished up to the nines until they shone again. But why three pairs as none were ever re-issued? The wonders of Whitehall!

We were called out one night. In the light of the moon someone had seen parachutes dropping 'over Beckbury way'. Prearranged positions were taken up and the night wore slowly on with everyone becoming increasingly bored and tired. Suddenly a shot rang out! Action at last! Everyone was electrified. Complete with escort the Company Commander strode away in the direction of the shot. A sentry had been posted along a narrow lane and he was asked, 'Did you fire that shot?'

'Yes Sir'.

'What at?'

'At a rabbit, Sir.'

'You absolute so-and-so!'

'Yes Sir, but I did as you instructed. I said halt but he came on. I said halt again and he took a few more hops forward. I challenged a third time and he still came on so I shot him.'

He had the rabbit to prove it too! That particular sentry was an elderly and altogether remarkable character with, I need hardly add, a most wonderful sense of humour. Not bad shooting either when you stop to consider it.

◇◇◇◇◇◇◇◇◇

25

THE WINTER OF '39

With its bitter frosts and heavy falls of snow, the winter of '39–'40 was said to be the most severe since 1894. In early February a sudden change brought a quick thaw accompanied by prolonged heavy rain. Ground had been so deeply frozen that water was unable to soak away and ran off the fields in rivers. There was severe flooding everywhere and the Severn rose at an alarming rate. Areas never previously affected were under water and in the village both the *Hundred House* and village shop were flooded. Severe frost struck again! The Severn steadied and its level gradually subsided. Had that not been the case there must surely have been a disaster for precious little daylight remained between its waters and the arches of the Bridgnorth bridge.

Later a driving drizzle of frozen mist covered everything with a thick coating of ice. Countless trees had large branches snapped off by the sheer weight of it and road conditions were simply chaotic. At Burwarton the damage to timber was so extensive it resembled a war zone, a sad and costly sight. Walter Eley, the Head Keeper there at the time, later told me that they picked up partridges which had been frozen stiff and encased in that clinging mist of ice.

Huge flocks of pigeons ruined fields of kale and brassica crops. There was a continuous cannonade of shots and thousands must have been killed. I knew of one farm where pigeons were actually being driven backwards and forwards from field to field to try and save crops but all to no avail. They simply stripped everything. In every garden they were sitting on top of sprouts and greens and were too weak even to attempt to fly away. Needless to say birdlife generally suffered grievously.

Anxious moments. He's pretty reliable but you can never quite trust these humans.

◇◇◇◇◇◇◇◇◇◇

26

FORTIES RECOLLECTIONS

Two or three years in the mid-Forties stand out for a number of reasons. For one thing we enjoyed glorious summers, a factor closely associated I suspect with the return of several species which had been missing for a number of years. For instance the redstart reclaimed his territory on the sandstone cliff at the back of the house and several other pairs were spotted in their old haunts. Nightjars also returned and their 'churring' on the park railings recalled many a youthful hour spent stalking that elusive sound for a glimpse of those mottled night hawks.

But glory of glories, a stroll in the last hour of the gloaming one evening late in May, a solitary woodcock roding the same regular beat over Spring Coppice, the same monotonous call 'churr–churr–churr–croak', then suddenly, clearly sweet and melodious from Brown's Covert beyond the Severn the liquid notes of that master songster. I went indoors and called the family out and we listened enthralled far into the darkness of that balmy May evening.

Which is the greater songster, a mature cock blackbird or our small sombre friend? That is something I have never quite been able to decide. So often during the day his voice is lost in the background of the massed chorus but at night when the stage is left to him he rises to new heights. It was good to know those sweet fluting notes of the nightingale were part of our country-side once again.

Another welcome return during the mid-Forties was that of the humming bird hawk moth. Surely they are one of the most beautiful creatures to grace the hour when a summer's day gives way to a summer's night. With the easing of wartime restrictions it was again possible to obtain flower seeds and we had grown an excellent patch of zineas which proved to be the great attraction.

During these years odd coveys of quail were reared on the estate. They had always made intermittent appearances which had invariably coincided with the better partridge years. I have not seen one, nor have I heard of any being seen in the neighbourhood since the early Fifties.

One day whilst watching the binder complete the final few rounds of a field at Harrington a family of corncrakes flew out. They were strong fully grown youngsters and this again was during the immediate post-war period. Hope was kindled that this beautiful bird might be coming to terms with modern farming techniques and would once again grace our cornfields. Alas that hope was to be quickly dashed and I heard my last solitary corncrake in a field fronting the house in '63, a lapse of some fifteen years. Since '63 there has been neither sight nor sound of one.

As you will have gathered earlier in these writings anything with a yellow jacket, black stripes and hot feet awakens a particular kind of dread, or to express it less kindly, a sheer blue funk in me! Small wonder that one of those Forties summers was indelibly printed on my mind by a big build-up of colonies of hornets. This occurrence stands out as being especially remarkable because it was the only time we ever had these unwelcome guests. Twelve nests were known to me on the estate and of course there must have been many others. In a huge old oak close to the house there were two.

A clump of young elm poles some six to eight inches in diameter stood in the wood behind the slaughter house. A path ran within a few feet of them and one day two or three hornets were seen clustered on one of them some feet above the ground. Within a day or so they had cleared a square inch or two of bark and were collecting the rising sap. Other areas of bark were removed not only from the original, but also from adjoining poles as more hornets joined the original trio. Within a week between twenty and thirty of these black and amber beauties were to be seen there throughout the day together with a host of moths, flies and lesser insects all attracted to the feast.

For the moths in particular it was a risky snack as every now and again a hornet seized one of them and flew away to their nest some fifty yards across the pit hole. Some of those moths were really large fellows but this was no deterrent. They were seized and borne away like their smaller brethren with no apparent sign of effort on the part of their captor. Flies were another matter, speed of eye and reaction their key to survival. As my brother so often remarks, 'There are but two species in nature--- the quick and the dead'! To our utter amazement some of those poles were killed by this insect activity.

When the hornets finally evacuated their nests that autumn a number were to be seen crawling up window panes after the lights were switched on. An outside light by the back door attracted still more and those fellows could be a little disconcerting if zooming around just above your head. During the following Spring I shot a number of young queens as they flew around the chimney stacks on the house. Clearly they fancied those chimneys, or even worse the attics, as a nesting site and the thought of that great oval comb was just too much for my nerves.

One Saturday during the early War years I met Walter Eley in Bridgnorth. He was the Head Keeper from Burwarton and he told me of the arrival of a newcomer to the district. A Canadian gent with a grey coat, a fine bushy tail and a breathtaking ability as a tree-climber. Just a few months later one of the keepers arrived at the door with the first grey squirrel shot on the Apley estate.

How different in character from our own native reds. A handsome animal it is true, but with the habits of a rat. It is now some thirty-odd years since that first grey was seen in Apley woods. Their numbers increased at an alarming rate and, sad to relate, there was a corresponding decrease in our native reds at the same time. Within so short a time the latter were extinct in this locality and it is more than a decade since I last saw one.

It is thought the reds were killed off by the greys. This I believe and accept for where the grey squirrel has taken over, which unfortunately is most of the country, the reds have vanished. I never actually witnessed this vast destruction either by fighting or the discovery of bodies and cannot recall anyone who has done so. My own belief, though I must stress I have no actual evidence to support it, is that the greys destroyed the reds by taking young from the dreys. On at least two occasions we found baby reds dead on the ground during that period of the first arrival of the greys. There could, of course, have been many other reasons for their death but from close observation of the habits of the grey this could well be an explanation.

For the forestry staff they are a major problem, being accountable for thousands of pounds worth of damage to growing timber. Their diet seems to be anything and everything, young sycamore and beech poles being particularly susceptible to them. In the early Fifties a squirrel club was formed in an effort to reduce this pest which had established itself in such numbers. Since then approximately five hundred have been destroyed annually by the combined efforts of club and keepers. Sectional aluminium rods are used to push dreys out of trees. Their occupants lose no time in baling out and can be shot by waiting guns.

In the Autumn of '72 unusually large numbers of jays were noticed. It was stated in *The Field* that there had been a large migration from the continent. Numerous pairs were still to be seen in the Spring Coppice the following Spring. These I was able to observe and they certainly did nest, but surprisingly they produced no youngsters. After leaving the nest their presence is well advertised by their squawking cries and it is difficult not to be aware of them. Could our friend the grey squirrel have been responsible for the dearth of young? Somehow I rather suspect he was.

Joe Jay, that colourful comedian of the woods. I confess to a great liking for the bad old villain, an epicure in the choice of so varied and mixed a diet, delicacies unfortunately often leading to his undoing. He has a fondness for eggs, especially those beautiful blue ones of the thrush and his day is really made by the find of a nest of rich brown pheasant eggs. A mimic supreme, even outclassing the starling, his imitation of the owl's low crooning notes are perhaps his masterpiece. His clowning antics whether on the ground or in a tree and uncertain erratic flight distinguish him from all the other denizens of the woods and open spaces and he is quite at home in both.

Whilst living in Norfolk my brother picked up two fledglings which had come to grief and took them home to rear. When mature one escaped and evaded recapture though he remained around the house for many days. Both had learned to speak a few words. For several years the remaining one thrived and was greatly prized. His vocabulary increased greatly and he was housed behind wire netting at one end of a scullery which was given over to the bird's comfort.

When my brother and his wife moved from Norfolk to the Via Gellia in Derbyshire Joey went with them and his abode became that house of tufa near the thermal spring which has never been known to freeze. His showpiece was a rendering of the song '*I Passed By Your Window When The Roses Were Red*'. What followed after that I quite forget but Joey sang it through clearly and without mistake until the last line which he always ended with 'Good morning, good morning Joe Jay!'

A road ran past the house and often when a heavy lorry was approaching he used to call out 'Ted's coming' then give vent to a real hearty laugh as the vehicle passed by. If it was indeed Ted's car he waited until it was in the yard then repeated 'Ted's here, Ted's here, Ted's here' several times without laughing. He used to chatter away for hours, fortunately not in jay language all the time, and was interviewed and reported in the national press.

When he finally died at a ripe old age there was a feeling of real loss. How strange though are the twists of fate and fortune ,for a short time later Kit, my sister-in-law, died tragically after a brief illness. It was well that Joey the mimic supreme was gone too, otherwise her voice and sayings would have lived and echoed on in that house of tufa.

Those years of the late Forties and early Fifties are memorable for yet another reason: those wonderful hatches of mayfly on the Worfe. We frequently fished the Higford and Crowgreaves stretch which were approached through a field known as The Bonemill. How often odd mayflies met us at the gateway some 300 yards from the river. Mayfly hatched in their thousands and the air was simply filled with them.

That short two weeks of the mayfly rise was perhaps the cream of the fishing. Certainly large trout again became surface feeders and the opportunities of making a good bag of sizeable fish was most pleasing and enjoyable. But after the feast, the famine. In the ensuing weeks fish were both hard to find and difficult to take. After a hot summer's day, late evening could often prove rewarding and yield the odd brace or so.

Personally I would rather fish the smaller flies and wonderful rises of blue duns and olives frequently afforded great sport. My best trout from the Worfe was taken on the Rindleford stretch a hundred yards upstream of the road bridge and weighed two and a quarter pounds. He was not taken on a mayfly but during a wonderful hatch of blue duns. Towards the tail end of the mayfly

I frequently fished an alder with pleasing results.

I look back and in so doing know those hours spent on the Worfe were some of the best of my life. I recall the barn owl with its nest on the Badger side floating over the rushy bottoms and averaging a kill every twenty minutes or so. Those drumming snipe, the mallard, teal and heron, the rookery in Badger woods and a host of smaller birds, so many of them migrants all feasting on that wealth of fly-life hatching from that pleasant stream. A beautiful spot if ever there was one!

Before leaving it, a little incident worth relating. A fish was rising upstream of the overflow and striking too hard I left my hackled mayfly in him. Whilst tying on a fresh fly there was another rise in the self-same spot. That fish grabbed my new fly first time over him. He was a half pounder and with two hackled mayflies in his mouth. Certainly in his case the hook had caused neither pain, nor for that matter any apparent inconvenience!

Before leaving those fascinating Forties a word on the reptile population. For a year or two there was a fantastic, and in my experience, totally unprecedented increase in snake numbers. Grass snakes and slow worms were everywhere. Some were killed by traffic on the roads and many were found in gardens in the village where they had never been seen previously. We had one in the cellar, his dried-up remains being found later during the winter months. Numerous cast skins lay beneath the park deer fencing where the bottom rail had been used to assist in levering the old skin from the snake's body. On woodland paths and rides where once the odd one would have been spotted, always an event of some considerable interest, it became commonplace to see three or four. After a year or so their numbers returned to normal. How often we found their eggs when digging for worms in the muck heap behind the cart shed as lads.

On only one other occasion do I recall such a completely unusual increase in a wild population. That time it was the shrew.

We had just started to rear pheasants again and a batch had been moved to a wood on Bromley Banks. It was simply alive with them and Jim Pryke picked up several well-grown poults which had choked to death trying to swallow them whole.

27

◇◇◇◇◇◇◇◇◇

WHAT A MAN

Another incident stands out from those years of the early Forties. For me, recalling it still arouses a pang of horror. At about 3am on a wintry November night I was woken by the telephone. Chaplin had been shot by a poacher in Patmarsh wood.

Believe me, no time was lost in getting over there! Between us his son and I carried the old man to his home where he died a few hours later, mercifully without regaining consciousness.

Bill Chaplin, 'Old' Chaplin as he had come to be known and referred to with a deal of affection, had been officially on the retired list for a number of years but, with all the younger keepers in the forces or engaged in war work, he had continued to look after the beat.

At two o'clock on a bitterly cold winter's night he heard shots in Patmarsh wood, his wood, and at the age of 82 he got up from a warm bed, called his son and they went out to tackle a poacher.

In attempting to express my own feelings I can do no better than quote the comment of P.C. Layton, our local bobby, later that morning. So very apt and remembered clearly to this day. 'Talk about devotion. Talk about loyalty. It just defies belief!'

What a tragedy.

What a man!

28

THAT WINTER

That arctic winter of 62/63 is not easily forgotten. Patmarsh beat had been let and for the early months of '63 was without a keeper. Every other day Ken Ray and myself fed game round the beat. We used to divide at the house, one of us feeding the wood, the other feeding partridges and the smaller spinneys and coppices. In a field at the bottom of Patmarsh lane ten rows of sugar beet still remained in the frozen ground. Only the tips of their leaves protruded through the crust of crystallised snow and somehow gave life to numerous species of birds, pigeons, pheasants, partridges, usually wild duck as well as many species of smaller birds.

Through those woods the most striking feature was the deathly silence and total absence of birdlife, apart of course where we scattered food for the game. After snow, birdlife is usually most noticeable in woodland but arctic conditions had prevailed for weeks and small birds had left *en masse* to seek food and shelter around farmyards and buildings. Disturbed by my looking over a wall into a piggery one day a vast cloud of them rose into the air. There was a host of species, even water fowl and pigeons.

With water hens frozen out from the ponds becoming an easy prey, not to mention the numerous frozen corpses, foxes were far from starving as was stated in the press at the time. Duck were frozen out from reservoirs, lakes and ponds and there was a huge influx of many different species onto the Severn. One wondered just how they managed to survive for goodness knows it looked cold and forbidding enough. At night many of them flighted to a field at Bromley where the only visible food was tips of stubble showing above the snow. Going through the lower Terrace one day, numerous mallard rose from the roadside where they had paddled and disturbed the snow. It seemed impossible that they had found beech mast, the husks maybe, but they had certainly found something.

One would have thought that of all the birds the lark family, those inhabitants of the windswept fields, would have fared particularly badly. Unbelievably that was not so for after the thaw their numbers were as great as ever. Of the three winters disastrous for bird life, two of them occurring in the Forties, I really believe that the one of '62/63 was the most destructive. In fact it is only during this last few years that some of the species which suffered most have regained their numbers. Hedge sparrow, wren, long tailed tit and little owl to mention but four.

◇◇◇◇◇◇◇◇◇

29

DAWN ON ACORN HILL

How often have I enjoyed the variety and volume of the dawn chorus whilst sitting on the seat at the extreme point of rising ground known as Acorn Hill. It overlooks both the parkland below and woodland curving away to the left. Why Acorn Hill I never knew, for the majestic mature timber is mainly Spanish chestnut and beech. There are clumps of rhodies and box-bushes, the latter a favourite nesting site of bullfinches.

As night gave way to early dawn, the perfect peace and quiet was broken, usually by a rooster from a distant cottage closely followed by a gentleman who was probably the last to retire the previous night yet is always an early riser. There is a glimpse of the flopping flight and a not unmusical caw as he crosses an opening in the trees. A distant cuckoo calls from across the parkland below, a twitter of robin's summer song, blackbird's liquid notes, a thrush and by then the awakening of another day, a free-for-all and all join in! Jenny wren's sweet ditty, so great a sound from so small a creature, the little bird fairly vibrating with the effort, a challenge to be bravely repeated again and again from but a few short paces away.

From no great distance there is the incessant chatter of jackdaws, a right old barny and racket from them. All the time a pair or two with nearby nests are floating round and round, at times looking as though they mean to come right over you but always swinging away just beyond gunshot range. Yes, the jacks know a thing or two! There is the cooing of countless woodies, cooing it seems until the old wood almost rings with the sound. A rustle amongst the dry leaves and the beady little eyes of a field mouse look you in the face, then not liking what he sees is gone with a whisk and a rustle.

With strengthening light, objects become more clearly defined. Chestnut Coppice beyond the Severn no longer a distant blur, but now clearly seen as a background to the beautiful scene emerging below. White mist drifting from the river, lifting in the gentle breeze, full of promise for a fine day. A kestrel hovering over the Long Hill dips and rises, to stand again, swings curving away, then hovers once more and is finally lost to sight behind the hill. Numerous deer on a hillside and in the distance a faint mew is heard as a buzzard joins in the quest for food.

From my vantage point, permitting a view down The Terrace the sky is full of movement over the high tree tops. There is still a chorus of bird song but it is fast giving way to the daytime calls and twitterings as morning unfolds and the business of the day gets under way. As the sun gains strength its warmth is a comfort for the early morning air was chilly.

A pleasant place to be, whatever the time of day!

30

FEATHERED RECOLLECTIONS

Migration has always fascinated me. Salmon, seatrout, eels, butterflies, not to mention the feathered hosts which spend summer or winter with us swelling and enriching our resident stocks.

All the annual migrations are breathtaking to say the least, but to me they are no more intriguing than those which take place on a local plane, particularly during the winter months as flocks are continually forced to seek out and switch to new feeding grounds.

Early one bitterly cold November morning I went to Astol Farm to shoot pigeons. They had been feeding on a clover ley in their hundreds. From where I built my hide there was an unbroken view of the surrounding countryside. There was a small stream wending its way through several little coverts spaced at intervals along its length and beyond them a large wood. It was a rough boisterous morning with a strong wind, a perfect day in fact for shooting pigeons.

After a considerable wait I finally spotted a small flock flying very low, almost at ground level. Their flight followed the line of the stream and I was able to watch them until they were lost to view beyond the large wood. This flock was followed by others, some large in number, others but a few. Over a period of some three hours I was fascinated by this migration in which there were some thousands of birds. By no means was it continuous; some breaks lasted only a few minutes, others as long as a quarter of an hour.

Given a strong wind a pigeon's flight is never level. Even when flying very low they continually dip and rise in response to its vagaries. Each of the packs I was watching, whether in hundreds or merely twos and threes, followed a line identical to that taken by the first flock deviating not one iota. Few, if any, of these packs could possibly have seen the one ahead.

So much for my morning's shooting as not one pigeon came within range. But I had no regrets; the opposite in fact. This uncanny sense of guidance and direction is indeed a mystery and a fascinating one at that. Why, on that particular morning, should every bird in that vast flock follow a new and hitherto un-travelled line of flight to another feeding ground probably several miles distant? How did they even know of its existence? Call it flock instinct, call it flock behaviour, call it what you like, but to me it provided irrefutable evidence that birds can, and do, communicate most effectively between themselves.

Other similar events spring to mind. How many times when shooting pigeons over kale during snowy spells have I known sport to cease abruptly following the onset of a thaw many miles away. On these occasions birds were invariably to be seen flying at great height to new feeding grounds, again at intervals and clearly beyond sight of each other. It all gives pause for much thought and wonder.

Now to another aspect of the feathered tribe, one which never ceases to surprise and please. Watching Old Nog the heron beating slowly homeward as dusk approaches, who could possibly guess at the fantastic display of aerial gymnastics he can turn on at nesting time? Again our friend the buzzard, so graceful when soaring, so ponderous in normal flight, yet with unbelievable speed and power in his stoop and dive. Not long ago I watched an outstanding performance by yet another unlikely character.

Whilst motoring slowly down a lane in the spring of the year, a kestrel preceded me, settling on one telephone pole, then flying on to the next each time I caught up with him. From a nearby strip of woodland a magpie appeared, made straight for the hawk and tagged on a mere foot or two behind him. There followed a display I could scarcely believe I was watching. No matter how the kestrel twisted, turned or dived, that magpie was always within a foot or so of his tail. That display lasted for a full ten minutes until they finally broke away. It amazed me that a magpie could attain, let alone sustain, the speed and agility these two birds displayed. At no time was there any attempt at aggression. Times without number I have watched chases involving nearly any species you may care to mention but never have I seen a comparable exhibition.

On the drying green stands a huge old holly tree which is laden with berries most winters. Seldom does it fail and for more years than I care to remember we have derived infinite pleasure from the hosts of birds which have feasted off it in such variety and numbers.

Years ago it was not unusual to see a score of hawfinches fly out of it and go dipping into the wood below. It is a long time since I saw so much as a single one for they have simply disappeared. Can our friend the grey squirrel know anything about this? During Ted Cooke's first year as beat keeper I went into his hut on the rearing field to find him feeding a baby hawfinch which had fallen from the nest. An amusing sight it was too for it had a comical way of swaying its head from side to side and emitting a plaintive little squeak at each beat. Anyway it thrived and was successfully reared on a diet of soaked biscuit meal and hard boiled egg.

During the winter of 1971-72, fieldfares stripped the holly tree in just two days and the ground beneath was smothered with berries which had fallen. Having cleared the tree they turned their attention to the ones beneath it. A prettier or more interesting sight than a couple of hundred fieldfares milling around, packed like sardines and gobbling up berries, it would be difficult to imagine.

Surprisingly there was not a single redwing sharing in the feast. In previous years they had always been there in force with the fieldfares. This winter ('74) great numbers of both fieldfares and redwings arrived in the Autumn but quite amazingly and, for the first time ever, the old tree was left completely alone by the invaders.

In many ways our Autumn bird migrations are far more interesting than the Spring ones. For one thing the latter are so much less obvious. In the space of a few short weeks they have arrived, so very welcome it is true, but the presence of the majority denoted more often than not by sound rather than sight. It seems the Autumn migrations are maintained but I am certain that is not so with the Spring ones. It may be that I do not hear so acutely or perhaps I fail to see so well or as quickly. That could certainly be true for the smaller species such as chiff-chaffs, warblers and whitethroats which are mostly woodland birds and so easily missed.

For the more obvious species the decline is alarming. Fewer cuckoos arrive each year. So far this year I have heard but one and have yet to see him. Only yesterday I had a letter from my brother saying he thought the cuckoo had forgotten to come this year. Swifts, swallows and martins get fewer each year. Food must come into it. These last few years the nightingale is again missing. These periodic breaks do occur though and we hope for his return.

So many of the rarer species have dwindled or gone. No corncrake with disconcerting call so difficult to place. Red backed shrikes whose nests and larders we found in the Spring Coppice year after year are greatly reduced. Last summer I caught a glimpse of a bird with a flattish flight; it could have been one. If so it was a hen. As mentioned earlier, hawfinches are completely missing.

When we were boys we found several nests of the nightjar and could listen to them churring away when lying in bed. In fact they were a common bird. One wonders whether the vastly diminished moth population has anything to do with their current scarcity

During our early years at Apley my brother was privileged to observe a hoopoo in the Spring Coppice. Twice I scored with a golden oriel, the first occasion a fleeting glimpse but enough to leave a lasting impression of beauty. On the second occasion it was an even briefer glimpse but his repeated musical call away in the top branches of tall oaks was unmistakeable. All travellers, just resting and then moving on. Not so the wryneck which used to nest regularly in the Spring Coppice. Never an easy bird to spot, it is true, but as lads we found their nests on several occasions, a hole in a rotten stump a foot or so above ground level being a favourite site.

Whilst some species have declined there has been a vast increase in others particularly our friend the starling. Strangely enough those huge flocks which roosted in their scores, indeed hundreds of thousands, have not been with us this year. Has there been a catastrophic decrease in their number or have they changed their feeding areas?

In previous years flocks converged on their roosting quarters from all directions. Some of those flocks were several hundred yards wide, at least fifty from front to rear and created a noise like the roar from a train as they passed overhead.

Two years ago they roosted in a wood called Barker's Rough which consists of mature timber. This was unusual as younger plantations and osier beds are usually preferred. As they prepared to roost an amazing spectacle unfolded. Thousand upon countless thousand took off from the nearby fields where they had been resting and had actually blackened, such were their numbers. This was but the preliminary to the evening display of their roosting flight. Zooming, rising and then dipping, now curving away from the wood for quite some distance, now returning to it and all the time new flocks arriving and swelling the countless host, a quite breathtaking display of precision flying, each lightning twist and turn executed as one.

Some years earlier they had chosen to roost in a plantation of young trees on Higford Banks. A shoot was arranged to try to save the trees and proved totally ineffective. At one stage there was tier upon tier in the air and so vast were the numbers it is no exaggeration to say the sky was darkened by them. Finally they were persuaded to move on by the forestry staff who kept fires going all night by burning old tyres or anything else that gave off noxious fumes. A plantation can quickly be destroyed and the stench is appalling. Once settled in on the trees, though, the term a 'murmuration' of starlings is brilliantly descriptive.

Rook and jackdaw populations have greatly increased. Rookeries are not shot out to the extent they used to be and the jacks are left entirely alone. Back to our boyhood days: if we saw seagulls, and we rarely did, we used to say that rough seas had driven them inland. Today every district is infested with them. Whenever ploughing is being done, the freshly-turned furrows are white with them, worms by the score going down their hungry gullets; surely not a good thing as worms are extremely beneficial to the land?

The laugh of the green woodpecker, known locally as the 'yaffle' is said to be a sign of rain. Perhaps the most arresting woodland sounds are the penetrating noise of drilling by his greater spotted cousin and drumming of his lesser spotted one. From the sweet song of Jenny wren to the bad old carrion's harsh croak, nothing is discordant. Amazingly they all seem to fit into the enfolding restfulness of woodland. Not so the night sounds! Contrast the dog fox's staccato bark thrice repeated and vixen's screech, hedgehog's scream and that eerie cry from the water hen flying high in the darkness.

To watch the amazing speed and ruthless savagery of a sparrowhawk striking a bird in mid-air is indeed to witness nature in the raw. What is not generally realised though is that a great proportion of their prey is taken at ground level, most probably on the ground itself. A sparrowhawk's control and speed of twisting flight in pursuit of its prey, even through dense undergrowth, has to be seen to be appreciated.

Once when shooting pigeons in Long Pool wood I was screened by a thicket of box bushes. A sparrowhawk flashed through them at terrific speed giving chase to a blackbird which it struck to the ground but a few feet away from me. So intent was it on its prey that it was completely unaware of my presence. Jimmy Reece told me he once killed one with his stick as it darted past him, again in pursuit of a blackbird through low bushes.

Without doubt the blackbird is their staple diet. That little tell-tale bunch of dark feathers so common on woodland rides or in hedge bottoms is proof in itself. Wood pigeons are thought by many to be their main diet. Each kill is left so strikingly obvious by the great scattering of light coloured feathers, so eye catching in contrast to the unobtrusive little bunch from the blackbird which is very easily missed. Certainly woodies are captured, usually by the larger hen, but even then I believe many are damaged or sick birds.

Some years ago a pair of swallows started to build a nest in the corner of our bedroom window. It was screened by the curtain and when first discovered was in the early stages of construction. It seemed a shame to pull it out so we decided to leave well alone and watch events unfold. A droppings board was fixed beneath the nest and sheets of strong brown paper laid on the floor beneath the curtain rail where the birds roosted.

We had a lot of fun and many surprises, perhaps the greatest being that they took no apparent notice and showed not the slightest alarm when the light was switched on, or for that matter when we moved around in the room.

It was Coronation year and the local celebrations were ruined by a lashing downpour driven by a bitter wind. We returned that night to find the hen on the nest and the cock a foot away on the curtain rail. Just as we were about to switch off the light a large brown moth floated in through the open window. Immediately the cock showed a lively interest following its every movement as it fluttered about the room.

To our surprise several minutes elapsed before he dived from his perch and we were still more surprised by the time it took him to make his capture. We could only conclude the bird was baffled and frustrated by the artificial light as this whole perform-ance was in such total contrast to the deadly accuracy displayed in daylight. Returning to his perch with the moth in his beak he gave several great gulps. With each one the moth was drawn a little further in and finally disappeared. Even then several more gulps were needed as the insect passed down the bird's throat.

We waited some time and sure enough another moth of similar size wandered into the room. A repeat performance! After a much longer wait another of these large fellows drifted in, but the entertainment was over for it was completely ignored. As may be imagined, moths were forever coming into the room through the open window. Only on that particular occasion was there ever an attempt to catch them. That rain-lashed Royal day had denied them their normal fare.

This story reminds me of another occasion when a barn owl settled on railings fronting the house. A mouse held by its head dangled from its beak. For quite some time he remained motionless, then a gulp and the head disappeared. Another pause, another gulp and down went most of the body. There was nothing hurried about that meal for there was yet another appreciable wait before the remaining body and tail went sliding out of sight. A flutter of his feathers and he floated away.

31

FEEDING THE FIVE THOUSAND

There is something which never ceases to amaze and mystify me. From late autumn, and into the winter months, nearly all the autumn migrants, together with our own similar species of home bred birds solve their food problems mainly from the open fields. Close to where I live in Shropshire there is a field known as The Big Turf. Week in week out, month after month, it is alive with feathered life giving sustenance to thousands of hungry birds. Starlings as usual in great numbers, together with flocks of pigeons, rooks and jackdaws; not to mention the hosts of fieldfare and redwing, mavis, thrush and blackbird.

Flocks of the lovely lapwing, at times rising and wheeling around the field, drift down again to settle once more in their characteristic feeding habit of a little run, a pause and a peck. There is the raft of golden plover some hundreds strong, similar in so many ways to their cousins and just as restless, often in the air and at times leaving the field. Never all together, but in small packs of a dozen or so, their straight fast flight taking them to fields about a mile away at the New House farm. Strangely it is rare to see them on any other fields in the district. Distinctive in flight their piping cry is of the fells and moorland. Apart from larks in great number, there are few of the smaller birds.

Day after day the bountiful feast continues: something for the insect eaters, the clover eaters, for the grub and worm hunters, snail and larvae searchers: provision for all and to suit all tastes and needs. To me it is as great a miracle as the five small loaves and two fishes!

32

THE DOG SWEEP

In 1939 our son was given a black Labrador pup by Charlie Kyte from the Wren's Nest. As with Glen so many years before, his arrival had become the predominant interest in life, and as with Glen, expectations were surpassed. He was named Sweep and rapidly made himself at home. Of all the dogs I have worked, or indeed have ever seen, that one was the greatest game-finder of them all.

To watch him casting about, head held high, in a field of roots in search of a runner was an experience in itself. Anyone who knew dogs but was not familiar with this one would have had grave doubts. When he hit the wind and galloped away, often a very long way and still with head held high, they would really have begun to wonder. But that final drive in and pick up and the stylish retrieve which invariably rounded off his efforts remains firmly in my mind and that of anyone else who ever watched him and knew a dog.

No matter where or how a bird fell he invariably 'sank the wind' whilst approaching it. Only the very occasional dog does this but what an asset it is. In practice it ensured that he always approached his retrieve against any slight breeze there was and when a bird had dropped in cover and run unobserved he was able to hit the line yards earlier than if he had run directly to where the bird landed and then cast about. During those war and immediate post-war years that dog got through more work than one should ever ask of any two dogs.

In his later years, he developed into something of a 'pot-hunter's dream'. At that period I frequently had the odd few brace of pheasants to shoot and, labour being at a premium, usually undertook the job myself with only the dog to help. A likely path was walked with Sweep a few yards ahead of me. When the old boy stopped, nose in the air, one front paw raised, a knowing look, it was time to take notice. If he set off with steady determination through the inevitable briars, it was time to follow. No need to rush. He would stay well within shot until the bird was flushed and the rest was up to me. That nose saved me many a score of miles and I look back on those jaunts with supreme pleasure as perfect examples of the working partnership and understanding which can develop between man and dog.

33

◇◇◇◇◇◇◇◇

THE OPEN RANGE

Change like a river flows on, now rushing, now barely moving, yet always onward. Everything is subject to it and pheasant rearing is no exception. Only a decade ago most pheasants were reared by the traditional open method with hens as foster mothers. Today the method of rearing them has changed completely. This change has been hastened by, of all things, the absence of broody hens. With the disappearance of traditional farmyard and cottage flocks, broodies are no longer available in sufficient numbers to meet demand. Incubators are now used to hatch eggs and chicks are reared in brooders. They are fed a complete balanced diet similar to that used for turkeys and can thrive without access to any natural food. No need to enlarge on this as the method is well known and has so much in common with poultry rearing.

Looking back pre-1914 and on into the 1920s, the picture altered but little. For their first week of life, pheasant chicks were fed finely chopped hard boiled egg dusted over with barley flour. Just why it had to be barley I never did discover. A fine grade of biscuit meal was gradually introduced and the proportion of egg correspondingly reduced and finally discontinued. From the age of two weeks the fine biscuit was gradually replaced by a coarser grade and meat in the form of rabbit and greaves (dried meat) together with rice, hempseed, cut maize, wheat and chopped lettuce. Occasionally chopped spring onions were also added.

Biscuit had to be scalded, great care being taken to avoid sogginess; rabbits were boiled until tender as were the other ingredients.

A portable copper with a capacity of eight to ten gallons was standard equipment and hand-operated mechanical choppers were used. When blended together with a final dusting of barley flour and 'Pheasant Meal',(described as spice by its makers if I recollect correctly), this mixture produced an appetising food which was readily eaten. Correctly prepared it had a crumbly texture and a handful gripped firmly disintegrated on re-opening the hand. Additions were few, cod liver oil and extra 'Pheasant Meal' being added during cold and wet weather.

The 1920s saw our first big change when Messrs. Armitage of Nottingham introduced a complete food for dry feeding; a mixture consisting of dried egg, quite an assortment of dried seeds including hemp and linseed, crushed cereals and cut maize. Biscuit meal together with dried ant eggs and small dried flies more or less completed the formula, the whole being impreg-

The rearing field, 1898. Here pheasant food is being prepared.
Anything would be chucked in to supplement the corn including
rabbits and household left-overs.

The open range, with mothers in the coops and the poults nearly ready to move to the wood.

nated with cod liver oil. This was their No. 1 food to be fed the first few weeks. It was packed in greaseproof containers inside hessian sacks. No. 2 was a coarser grade with fewer eggs and flies and, I think, the oil discarded. No. 3 was an altogether coarser mixture. Feeding was carried out four times daily, the mixture being sprinkled on slates with a continuous supply of clean water and a pinch of fine grit daily. We found birds were satisfactorily reared, possibly with fewer losses, but growth was somewhat tardy and they feathered slowly.

During the 1930s Fairburn and Tullet of Rotherham introduced a food they called 'Dry-Soft'. Initially it was somewhat decried but soon gained ground and very quickly it was being used by the majority of rearers. Birds thrived and it was the nearest approach to a fully balanced diet up to that time. Most of the Armitage ingredients were retained but a liberal quantity of fishmeal was added to improve protein content and quality.

Taken stage by stage the process has been a gradual one and in order to bring its real magnitude into focus I would like to portray a typical day on the rearing field way back in the early 1920s:

Arriving at six o'clock in the morning, complete with a game bag full of conies, I would already have passed the time of day with the Home Farm waggoners bringing in the horses to prepare for a day's work. Jim White would have joined me at the gate into the rearing field and as we made our way through grass drenched with dew to the hut in its centre, we would have been greeted by the song of numerous larks. We had found several of their nests and marked them with pegs in order not to disturb them.

Food prepared the previous evening and graded for various age groups was all ready for the first feeding of the day. After breakfast the copper was got going, rice being cooked first, then maize, wheat and rabbits and finally the greaves and biscuit meal scalded. At the same time, coops were opened up and moved to fresh ground. Twice a week a pinch of flint grit was thrown to each one. At eleven o'clock a second feed was given to birds up to three weeks of age. At 2pm all were fed again, then for the last time at 6pm, after which cooking was repeated in readiness for next morning.

Finally coops had to be closed. Those housing young broods presented no difficulty, but older ones could often be exasperating in the extreme. It was not an atom of use beginning before they had settled for the night and after a hot day the shades of evening were fast closing in. Fortunately there was often a drop in temperature which helped and if accompanied by a breeze, then so much the better.

During the day, lids would have been carried well behind the coops and propped up to be seen more easily as night closed in. How often, just when reaching with the lid after a breath-holding approach, a little gent chose that precise moment to stroll out for a final look around. You froze and very occasionally he went back inside after a brief survey. More often than not though a few of his mates came out and joined him and you faded into the background hoping to goodness the coop would not empty and flush provoking a snowball eruption from its neighbours. Those were long days! Two hundred coops, and as a little make-weight four coops of turkeys for the Home farm, were reared on those 52 acres. Quite a few steps in the course of a day.

This method of rearing was open to attack by vermin and one's senses became attuned in an amazing manner. An alarm call from a hen or maybe a swallow, a scolding blackbird in nearby hedgerow, or a flush of frightened pheasants all called for rapid investigation. Prior to, and indeed throughout the time birds were actually on the field, the surrounding area was trapped. Rats and stoats were not usually difficult to deal with but if you were unfortunate enough to have a litter of weasels arrive and ensconce itself in mole runs, that spelt trouble. I have seen chicks pulled down and underground in a split second. Year in year out it always happened; a kestrel was to be seen hovering, then swooping down and away with a bird. If it was not got straight away it was soon going to account for many more.

A sparrowhawk was a different proposition. It simply swept into the field, picked up a bird and was away in a flash. Sometimes it returned after only an hour, or it could be a couple of days later, but of one thing you could be certain, return it assuredly would. By contrast the kestrel was persistent and fairly predictable. Rooks and jackdaws were often troublesome particularly during spells of hot dry weather. Keepers have come in for much criticism from bird lovers but this destruction was necessary on the rearing field. Unfortunate, but it was the only way to save pheasant chicks; without it, losses would have been counted, not in twos and threes, but in scores. In passing though I should point out that on a well-keepered estate you always found prolific bird and animal life including all the predatory species mentioned.

In this brief description I have only touched the fringe of the subject, but before leaving it I must say that I can think of few

H.Q. the Rearing Field. This was the centre of activity throughout Norman's 18-hour day.

things more fulfilling. Some of the happiest hours of my life were spent on a rearing field. Hatching, feeding and rearing those little balls of fluff you took to the open range had a fascination all of its own.

With the hen pheasant's guidance these little mites are able to sustain themselves in the wild immediately on leaving the nest. On the rearing field, the foster's warmth and devotion went far towards achieving the same result. How often have I watched them appearing out of their runnels through the long grass following the old hen's invitation to a meal. At least once a day, time was taken to observe them feeding and assure yourself all was well. Clear shining eyes, erect little tails, a sheen on their feathers - but again I am wandering and since this is not a treatise on pheasant rearing will leave it at that, albeit somewhat reluctantly.

Those chicks were given great scope on the open range. They learned to search out an abundance of food from both pasture and soil. From the age of a week they could make use of their wings. It was always a pleasing sight on a hot afternoon to see brood after brood lifting into the air and flying twenty yards or so before landing. Instincts had full scope to develop and with them an awareness of so many of the dangers they are exposed to. All these advantages are denied the modern system though as a means of providing sport it is proving successful. In many ways it is to be commended; yet to me the fascination and charm of the open range remains as strong as ever.

Over the last half century, great advances have been made in the diagnosis and treatment of disease. So little help was available in those early days. Game food manufacturers were to a great extent the only source of advice one could turn to. With a serious outbreak of disease and subsequent post mortem examination, how often the only advice received was to destroy all appliances used, coops, sitting boxes, in fact the whole jolly caboodle! At that time the range of modern drugs, preventatives routinely incorporated in the diet, or curatives available on request was simply undreamed of.

One season we had a disaster with an outbreak of B.W.D. (Salmonella). Losses were heavy, around 800, two long rows of coops being practically wiped out. Nearly at my wit's end I went to a chemist friend in Bridgnorth and asked him to make up a solution of quinine as strong as he dare which would not to kill pheasant chicks only a few days of age. This was mixed in their food. Whether or not it did have any effect I really cannot say, but after its use that particular outbreak quickly subsided.

Two final recollections of the open range. The first concerns those very early morning strolls when many miles were walked to get rabbits for feeding the young birds. They had to be old ones; why old ones I never knew! Just a preliminary to the day's work! With its acres of bracken, the park was the usual centre of activity and the actual shooting gave a deal of satisfaction and pleasure. Later in the year from about August and then on throughout the winter, twelve rabbits had to be got and sent to the Hall twice weekly, and of course – they had to be young ones!

The second recollection concerns a bicycle. During the period I was away at the war, my cycle had been hung up for storage and on my return it was rather rusty. At every odd spare moment on the rearing field Jim and I worked at it until it shone again. We decided to give it a coat of paint with extremely pleasing results. It really did look super. Finally the great moment arrived when it was wheeled out onto the road and mounted – and the front forks completely collapsed. That particular machine was called a Wearwell!

Gone to the woods – only when the birds were safely up to roost did the pressure on the keeper ease.

34

◇◇◇◇◇◇◇◇◇

UNHAPPY COINCIDENCE

Swans nested on a small island in the Long Pool for many years but the young never survived. They were successfully hatched out, then after a few days their number decreased and little more than a week later there were none left. Gazing through a window one day I saw a most amazing sight. I gave a shout and the rest of the household joined me. There they were. The cob, the pen and two surviving cygnets were on the road about fifty yards from the house. They had already travelled some two hundred yards from the pool.

They came on very slowly and finally reached the yard. Even in that short distance they had taken two long rests. After patiently waiting for their young to move on again the old birds crossed the yard and went through an open gate into the Spring Coppice. We all moved to the drying green where we could again watch them. It was quite obvious the cygnets were weak and very, very tired.

The Spring Coppice slopes down to the Severn and by an unhappy coincidence woodmen were working some hundred yards down the bank, their axes ringing out loud and clear. Clearly the parent birds were assessing the situation and it was equally clear that their opinions differed. Time after time the cob went forward and then returned to them. Then the two parent birds stood with arched necks bowing and touching each other. Finally the pen definitely decided to go no further and led the sad little procession back into the yard.

There they rested again before beginning their long trek back to the pool. It was not achieved without many more rests but they did finally make it. A day or two later the young were dead. It appeared the river was the goal they had to reach if they were to survive. One can only surmise they died of starvation, the pool being deficient in the necessary diet. I strongly suspect silkweed was the missing ingredient.

◇◇◇◇◇◇◇◇◇

35

OTTERS

What a fascination those otters held for me. How often I watched a pair fishing at the head of Gadstones. Again there were the litters reared below Browns. Throughout one memorable summer in particular they were much in evidence and added to the magic of many a gloaming.

Whilst fishing the head of the pool at The Roving one evening I saw what, for a few moments, I thought was the splash of a salmon some hundred yards upstream. There was no mistaking the second 'rise' some thirty yards nearer as an otter surfaced with that porpoise-like hump which was repeated at intervals as he worked downstream towards me. On one occasion he surfaced but a few yards from where I was wading. Next time I saw him he was down river and swimming back up towards me with an eel dangling from his mouth.

He left the water right opposite me and I watched him consume his catch which to my surprise was very quickly eaten. Again he entered the river, his trail of bubbles clearly seen. He fished the run down once more finally surfacing with another eel at the identical spot his first catch was made. This time he dined alone screened from me by the branches of a willow but only for a few moments! His stream of bubbles showed again in the water and I knew he had at last seen or winded me; why not before I simply cannot think.

Two incidents involving otters repeatedly spring to mind. As one approaches the river at Browns there is a slight promontory where many years earlier a grand old oak used to grow. Its branches spread far out across the water creating an ideal spot for dapping chub when those small green caterpillars of the oak moth were dropping. Whist assembling my rod on the site of the old oak I was startled by an otter smacking into the pool a few feet beneath me. Not that smooth soundless entry on this occasion but a resounding splash. Next day the same thing happened.

There was no visible holt and he must have been lying rough. Each time that fleeting glimpse left the impression of a shaggy coat and general roughness most unusual in an otter. Just a passing incident but how often I have wondered just what circumstances brought him there in that condition.

Fishing Brights down one morning I became aware of movement on the near bank. It was an otter snuffling through the herbage. Then for some time he nosed around my fishing bag which was lying on the ground. Finally he moved on up the river side, stopped to pick something off some sedges and then disappeared from view. That otter seemed quite oblivious to my presence. Whether or not he had indeed seen me I shall never know.

Later that morning I left Brights and crossed the river by the suspension bridge upstream to fish above Cox's island. A pair of long-tailed tits were making a great commotion. They are known locally as 'can-bottles' and their beautifully-made nest in a thorn bush was nearing completion. Sure enough it was our friend again and a few moments later I spotted him on the opposite bank. For several minutes he stopped to ruminate amongst a cluster of nettles in a little hollow and then continued on his journey upstream.

I had been told that a mating otter loses all sense of danger. In this case it could be the explanation, but after countless hours on the riverside I can recall no other similar incident and this chap seemed utterly out of character. Was it merely a touch of spring or was it something a little more sinister – yet another hint of things to come?

36

SEVERN SALMON

During the late 1920s there was a surge of interest in the potential of the Severn as a salmon river. Its claim as England's premier river had finished when Telford built the weirs.

Fish passes were in fact built into them but proved totally inadequate. Of the few fish still ascending the river, the majority managed by getting over the weirs in high water. Netting in the estuary and upstream, I believe as far as Tewkesbury, accounted for most fish caught. Few were taken by rod.

It was the local press which drew attention to the success being enjoyed by anglers fishing on the public water below the weir at Shrewsbury. Details of weights and numbers together with names of successful anglers were published weekly. A little further downstream, the Sentinel works owned a stretch of water in which their employees fished. Each week a family named Corbett recorded numerous fish. At that time it was said that sons with assembled rods met their fathers at the riverside where they had dashed on bicycles to fish out their dinner hour.

Riparian owners finally began to take notice of the river's potential. Efforts were made to curtail the extent of the netting. If I recall correctly these met with very minor success. Interest was further stimulated by the odd fish being taken in our own locality. Lord Forrester and General Ward on the Willey Estate water, Mr D'Arcy downstream of Bridgnorth and Sir Charles Grant at

Moving rocks to create salmon lies during low water conditions.

Atcham all recorded fish. Most successful was a rod called Norrey who fished the Ironbridge and Buildwas area.

Success did not always come without its price. Lord Forrester was playing a fish and Harry who was ghillying for him was nipping back and forth behind him in a state of high excitement. Harry had uncorked the gaff and as he ran past once more trying no doubt to spot the best place to land the fish he sank its point well and truly into his Lordship's backside. Describing the incident later Harry told me that what with swearing, trying to play the fish and clutch his injured buttock all at the same time it was some pantomime. Somehow though the fish was landed and whilst Harry attended to that side of things, the peer dropped his trousers to view the damage. Sure enough blood was streaming down his leg but the old boy began to laugh. 'I'll tell you what,' he said to Harry, 'I'll just tell you what my lad! It's a bloody good job for you we did get him out!'

It was against this background that in 1930 Mr Herbert Hatton from Hereford was engaged jointly by Lord Forrester and Major Foster to make a survey of their respective waters. His visit was favoured by a low water. He arrived at Linley station to be met by the Willey and Apley agents, Harry Cook, who at that time was water bailiff, and myself. It was well into the evening before we finished and partook of welcome refreshment in the Brewery Inn at Coalport.

In his report Herbert Hatton suggested positions for additional lies to be created. These were shown in clearly and cleverly drawn diagrams with detailed instructions regarding materials and methods. That day was a lucky one for me for it was the beginning of a friendship which ended only with Hatton's death.

In 1931 Bill Cox was engaged as part time ghillie and keeper. With a great team comprising Cox, George Wilkinson, Walter Price and Charles Wilding, the work of providing additional lies or lodges was completed in the summer months of 1931 and '32 when the river was running low. Two methods were employed: smaller rocks were unloaded from a flat-bottomed boat made at the estate yard. Larger ones were dragged into place using a monkey winch. Blocks of stone could usually be found on the banks where they were wanted. Originally they must surely have been blasted from the bed of the river to give clearance for the laden barges of former days as there were drill holes in many of them.

A short distance upstream of the suspension bridge a large slab of rock several tons in weight was being guided into position to divert the flow of water. A cable attached to the rock ran across the river to a pulley at the base of a large tree. The strain proved too great; the cable snapped and for a moment the river seemed to divide so great was the impact. A huge lamprey was swept into the side by the resultant wash and was captured by Walter Price. Barely a minute earlier two canoes had passed beneath that cable and were still in sight as this mishap occurred. In those days canoes were a rare sight on the Severn and someone had taken a photograph of them as they came downstream.

Apley lies on the middle reaches of the river. Long stretches of slower water or flats are interspersed with swift flowing runs or fords which form the main salmon pools During the early part of the season salmon are to be found on the flats where spinning provides the only opportunity of taking them. From April onwards fish start lying in the runs and the fly can contribute to the bag.

The Severn is an early river. Many times when walking its banks in January, or even in late December, I have seen springers and of course a fair number are taken below Shrewsbury weir in the opening weeks. On this stretch though, February is a lean month. A low settled water is our prime requisite for success and how seldom can I recall such conditions early on. A succession of little rises invariably frustrates all hope of a fish in the opening weeks or even months and it is in this context that records should be assessed.

Several of the heavy type of Scottish fishing boats were purchased and on 15th March 1933 Major Foster caught a salmon in the Apley waters. It was the first one in living memory. The Major took a second fish, but results were so poor that after persevering for some time he gave it up. Odd fish were still being taken here and there but it was at the Shrewsbury and Stourport weirs where all the fun was being had.

One amusing incident from this lean period: a fish had been seen at the lower end of Bright's run and Cox was rowing the boat for Sir John Milbanke. Sir John had taken a gun with him. Sitting down again after taking a shot at a high flying jackdaw out of Chestnut Coppice he picked his rod up and started to reel in. There was something on the end and after a brief fight the salmon won the day. Poetic justice no doubt, but so typical of the nigh unbelievable incidents which so often punctuate and enrich the sport of salmon fishing.

Moments before the cable snapped!

On 1st April 1933 I landed my first fish at Lower Severn hall. He was twenty-one pounds and taken by spinning. Herbert Hatton had made me a greenheart rod which I still use and after these many years it is nearly as straight as the day it was bought. He also sold me a walnut Nottingham centre pin reel, another true and faithful servant, with the glorious advice that, 'It would require mastering, but once achieved would contribute a degree of pleasure to spinning which is denied to those who seek the easier option' How very true, and for the sake of initiates to the art of spinning, how I wish that advice could still be imparted and accepted! That supreme pleasure of complete and direct contact with swinging bait, every move and twist of a hooked fish, these are never known through slipping clutches and gear ratios. But to cut the preaching and return to fishing! In May '33 I took a second fish at Bright's using an eighteen foot spliced fly rod.

For any season up until 1946 the total catch never exceeded four. Looking back on those years there can be no doubt our lack of knowledge was a severe handicap. There was so much to learn about the interplay of season and height of water, suitable sizes and patterns of lures and flies, fishing heights of various pools and all this against the background of a scarce quarry. Many an hour was spent in vain on lies which even today have yet to yield a fish. Notice I use the word spent and not wasted, for to me there is no such thing as the impossible lie or uncatchable fish. Once such beliefs take hold the challenge goes and with it the chance to turn many a blank day into something memorable. It has been hard learning, frequently frustrating. In terms of fish landed it could not even begin to bear comparison with the beats of famous rivers. Nevertheless the landing of a Severn salmon still provides a thrill, a sense of achievement denied to so many who have learned their fishing in surroundings where success is nigh a certainty.

But fishing is not just catching fish. Over the years a wealth of memories create a background against which catching of fish, the original driving force, becomes but a part. It is always a thrill to see the first of the migrant birds arrive: a sandpiper's flat flight over the water or chiffchaff unseen but heard nearby. One of the sweetest sounds I know are the bells, yes the bells, of St. Mary's, floating three miles upstream on a perfect May evening,

To land a Severn salmon is a very special thrill,
a real sense of achievement

a background to all the other beautiful sounds and melodies of that merry month. Music of rippling water, bleating of frisking lambs in the field beyond, even the old 8.15 puffing along, no real distraction but most pleasant to see and hear.

Those water meadows at Winscote held a great attraction for me. Scores of sand martins made the high sandy banks their nesting site. A kingfisher regularly fished The Cut, its trade mark a stall and hover before finally diving and hitting the water with that surprisingly heavy plop. Friendly breeding sows, so regular in their habits your watch could be set by them, a string of them making heavy going of it as they wended their way to a snug dormitory in the sandstone caves, once the sleeping quarters of the old time bargees.

But back to fishing. During those early years there was a total dearth of fish from June onwards. Not until the mid Forties did the odd report of June sightings begin to trickle in. 1949 brought the first June fish and almost unbelievably another one in July. '51 saw five caught in June and six in July. During the Fifties the increase in small summer fish became really noticeable. From a total of forty in '54 twenty-four were under ten pounds.

One memorable day in May '57 five fish were taken. At last it seemed the promise of the late Forties was being achieved. These small fish were clearly getting over the weirs on a low water and a feeling grew that the Severn salmon had finally come to terms with them. That miracle a few of us had dreamed of whilst plugging away at a beautiful but near empty river was finally going to unfold! Old Man Severn seemed poised to regain his rightful place amongst salmon rivers.

Turn now though to the records. Look at the decline in catches from the early Sixties onwards; a truly dreadful and unlooked for state of affairs. Apart from the fall in catches my diary referred with increasing frequency to the state of the river. To quote from notes made in '64, 'A very dry spring, good flushes later but when levels dropped to a fishing height a filthy amber colour prevailed in which fish neither took nor stayed.' Identical comments in ensuing seasons. As the water came into ply following a spate in past seasons it ran clear and good fishing conditions were enjoyed.

Years ago after the Severn had fallen inches below summer level I spent many an hour investigating certain submerged rock formations in the hope of finding a possible reason why fish did not take there. Given the right light they were visible many feet below the surface. I mention this in emphasising the amazing change which has taken place.

Eels could be watched in the shallows at the head of Brazier's and shoals of roach, their sides flashing as they flexed and fed on the algae and nosed into clean bright gravel. Wading down the runs a school of small fish was always to be seen easing down just in front of my feet. Occasionally, when idly turning a flat stone here and there it was easy to watch the loach dart away to seek shelter again amongst more distant stones and gravel.

The first 30-pounder, displayed on the drying green with Glen's kennel and the holly tree in the background.

TABLE OF ROD-CAUGHT SALMON FROM APLEY

	Feb	Mar	Apr	May	June	July	Aug	Sept	Av, Weight	Total
1933		1		1					19	2
1934										
1935			3						12	3
1936		2	1	1					16	4
1937-9										
1940		1							17	1
1941		1	1	2					19	4
1942		2							23	2
1943		5	2						18.5	7
1944		1							10	1
1945		1							21	1
1946		1	1						17	2
1947										
1948		4	5						12.5	9
1949				2	1	1			13	4
1950		2							14.5	2
1951		2			5				13	7
1952	3	2	8						15.5	13
1953		7	2						16.5	9
1954		12	14	13		1			10.5	40
1955		1	9						13	10
1956	2	5	16	5		6			12.5	34
1957		5	18	17					12.5	40
1958		8	17	4	4	5		1	13.5	39
1959	1	1	2	10	3				13,5	17
1960		5		2					14	7
1961		6	6		2				11	14
1962		1	4	2		1			10	8
1963		2	5			3	1		12.5	11
1964				2	5				1.5	7
1965						1			10	1
1966						1			6	
1967			1			1			13	2
1968-70										
1971								4	7	4
1972			1				7		7.5	8
1973			1						8	1
1974							2	1	7	3

Nowadays from spring until the floods of winter a greasy filthy slime smothers the river bed. To turn a stone over to see a loach results only in a cloud of sediment discolouring the water There is practically no fly life, hence no bird life. This last summer it has been possible, indeed almost pleasant, to sit of an evening after a hot summer's day without giving a single thought to the midge battalions which in previous years kept one swatting away with a bunch of comfrey. There is no other word for this state of affairs than pollution, and to a very marked extent.

Even the swans have forsaken the Apley waters. Until a few years ago nesting pairs successfully reared their broods on each of the islands. Not only the swans but also my friends the otter and water vole have gone, but more of them anon.

◇◇◇◇◇◇◇◇◇

HERBERT'S POST

Through Herbert Hatton we fished many beats on the Wye including his own at Bridge Sollars. No other shop has the friendly helpful atmosphere of the fishing tackle shop and one looked forward to each visit to Hattons. Herbert's fund of good stories and ready wit together with his vast knowledge of the Wye and its fishing lore were both entertaining and instructive. His lightning diagrams of the beat you were to fish were so descriptive and coupled with his advice gave us many a fish we would not otherwise have caught.

At the bottom end of Beat Six at Fownhowpe, a fence came down to the edge of the water. Herbert said, 'Drop your bait right at the foot of the bottom post. It will swim a few yards and become fast. It will shake off and travel another yard or two and be fast again but this time something will be tugging at the end!'

My brother fished the spot and that is exactly what happened. A good fish was on for a few minutes and then away. The day was fast closing in and we were still clean. I said, 'Let's go and give Herbert's post a final try.' Exactly the same thing happened but this time Ted landed his fish just as daylight was fading.

◇◇◇◇◇◇◇◇

A HAPPY MEDIUM

No pheasants were reared on the estate from 1939 until 1955. Over that period wild pheasants and partridges gave a lot of shooting, good seasons and some very bad ones. One year the total pheasant count was only around three hundred but quickly reached the thousand mark a year or two later. Small bags, small parties, some very indifferent shooting and yet looking back what pleasant days those were.

Gone were the euphoria and flamboyancy of the Twenties and Thirties. Great uncertainty regarding the very survival of the big estates, indeed shooting itself, was manifest for those were the years of Post War austerity and rampant Socialism. If those years served no other purpose I believe they did much to bring home the lesson that there is so very much more to shooting than the actual killing of game. Naturally they were not without their share of amusing incidents:

We had met at Higford and were walking a rough ferny bank towards the wood. A rabbit was started with a dog in close pursuit. Two shots rang out. Bunny went bobbing on but the dog rolled over and lay stretched out on the ground. Standing on top of the ridge I watched a ring of men gather round the prostrate dog, altogether a rather sad and pathetic sight. A voice said 'I can assure you I didn't shoot him, Boy. I can't have done. I'm only using number seven shot.' Another voice replied 'I am not for one moment suggesting you did, Joe, but I'm equally certain I didn't!'

At that point I shouted down to suggest someone make sure the dog was dead. Jim Pryke reached down to turn him over. I can still see his astonished face as he nearly fell over backwards, the dead dog erupting a good three feet into the air! Down he came and away he raced, his ears flapping as only a spaniel's can. He scattered a flock of poultry at one of the Higford cottages, careered away on and out of sight. It was the time hysteria was so prevalent, but he certainly chose his moment to throw a fit.

Following reintroduction of rearing in '55 bags gradually built up again and over the last ten years or so the main days have averaged around the two-fifty mark. There is no point in detailing individual shoots; suffice to say excellent shooting continued again giving pleasure to many people.

Comparison of past and present is a never ending source of argument. Probably in this respect I am as guilty as the next and to me, sport in all its various forms makes the most absorbing subject of reminiscence.

Looking back over the years, I recall periods before both World Wars when it seemed the dominating feature of the great estate shoots lay in recording the number of birds killed. Totals of four figures were common. On some of the best known shoots, Knowsley, Wellbeck, Elvedon, Hawkstone, Warter Priory, Hall Barn, Sandringham, Chatsworth, to name but some which spring easily to mind, many bags in excess of two thousand were recorded, the occasional day of more than three thousand, with the record standing at just under the four thousand mark.

So much has been recorded in relation to the outstanding perfection and merit of the great shoots of those times. They were superbly managed and conducted. It became common practice for pairs of guns to give way to threes; one standing to cool whilst the other two were in use. Whilst recalling those two distant peak periods we should keep in mind the huge numbers of birds reared and the guns who shot them. Many of those guns were shooting four or five days a week with the expectancy of firing several hundred cartridges each day. Prior to the pheasant shoots heavy bags of grouse and partridges were made. All this was intermixed with ground game abounding, days wildfowling, rabbit and snipe shooting. For anyone interested in numbers and records established during those times I can do no better than refer you to H.S. Gladstone's *Record Bags and Shooting Records*.

Looking back to those great bags preceding the two wars evokes no thrill in me. Superb organisation, two outstanding generations of head and beat keepers, superb marksmanship, but alas so many of those records made with easy birds flying straight and at no great height out of the flat woodlands which are a feature of so many of the more famous shooting counties.

To my mind it is a phase of sporting history which should be accepted and left at that. Future attempts to emulate it will be to the detriment of the sport. If six or eight men using single guns and loading for themselves cannot find supreme satisfaction in a bag of a couple of hundred quality pheasants then there is something sadly amiss. To suggest a figure is to stoke the fires of controversy, but to my mind this represents a happy medium, still the most difficult thing to achieve in life when all is said and done.

At the present time shooting remains more popular than ever. Apart from the landed interests there are shooting clubs and syndicates in practically every district. More pheasants are reared than ever before and the fact that shooting is shared and enjoyed by a far greater number of people from all walks of life is to my mind wholly excellent and bodes well for the future.

39

THE EVER-CHANGING SCENE

Looking from my home the skyline is cut by a stretch of stately woodland known as The Terrace. For several miles upstream of Bridgnorth its mighty oak and elm, its wonderful stands of beech and sweet chestnut adorn the eastern side of the Severn valley. It is an ever changing scene and each season projects its own image.

In winter towering red sandstone outcrops capped with stands of mature Scots pine and brakes of rhododendrons reassert a right of prominence, justly so for they certainly are eye catching! With leaf off the trees it is once again possible to catch a

A field of stooks in the 1940s, looking towards The Terrace.
The combine harvester was to change this farming practice forever.

fleeting glimpse of the riders of the hunt stringing along the grass carriageway on top of the ridge.

From mid-January, or maybe a little later, an almost imperceptible change commences. Leaf buds begin to swell, at first so very slowly, but as they do so the tints and hues intensify. Before the final emergence, a misty purple effect deepens each day; then suddenly a haze of delicate greens, olives and ochres rules in shades innumerable.

As fullness and richness of summer attain a peak of perfection a walk along those shady woodland paths reveals the urgency of spring giving way to more restful and lazy days. Bird song is still delightful though much reduced in volume. New voices are heard. There is the nest of young jays, oh so noisy, and now trying early flight from tree to tree: and all the other squeaking chirping youngsters to gladden the eye and please the ear.

So the year creeps on, promise of spring finally fulfilled in the acorn and nut-laden bounty of autumn days. Russet and gold predominate as leaves become tinted with a multitude of colours. This then the final beauty of the year, each individual tree and bush fitting into an intricate jigsaw of stunning colour. There can be no more descriptive name than 'autumn glory'.

For me, watching this timeless transition, this ever changing scene, year after year, season after season, for that matter day by day has been one great long ongoing pleasure. When one is old how easy to use the words 'I remember'. So often alas they precede unfavourable comparison! How pleasant then to record that all is well with this pleasant wood. Glorious stands of timber remain as mighty and graceful as when I was a small boy.

Scars of two world wars have been erased. Saplings replanted then and so pleasingly mixed are becoming sizeable trees. In years to follow they will become the majestic overlords of this woodland kingdom ensuring continuity of good forestry. The Terrace will continue to give life and sanctuary to a host of woodland creatures. It will fulfil its promise of beauty and fascination for generations to follow. For there is an air of permanency about a great wood: an air of peace, tranquillity and continuity which completely transcends the conflict and confusion of our own human lives.

Looking down the road to the Long Pool. A long plod for a baby toad, but they made it by the score.

◇◇◇◇◇◇◇◇◇

40

A PLACE OF GREAT BEAUTY

Parks are one of the glories of the English countryside and Apley was no exception. Although not one of the largest it was certainly a place of great beauty. Leaving the main entrance a delightful picture unfolded as one approached a valley where – in my boyhood days – fallow deer and Highland cattle held pride of place. Of the four hundred odd acres a hundred or more were covered by bracken. Across the valley were the deer-sheds, which gave their name to the surrounding area and immediately beyond was that glorious wooded escarpment known as The Terrace. The sheds nestled in a depression enclosed on three sides by sharply rising ground, the southern-most knoll topped by a wonderful stand of Scots pine. There can be few places where sunset creates a picture of so many shades and such great beauty. As autumn comes in colours and contrasts intensify and for one or two unforgettable evenings, as the sun slowly sinks and disappears, we see it at its very best.

With its three clumps of trees, Long Hill is perhaps the most prominent feature. It is still home to countless pairs of jackdaws. No year passed without a wild duck or two nesting on the flattish top of the hill, a long way from any water. Birds are not always wise in their selection of nesting sites! Long Hill once was simply honeycombed with rabbit burrows and on a summer's evening the hawk-like flight of nesting nightjars could always be enjoyed there.

A four foot wall of sandstone topped by a four foot iron deer fence divides Terrace from Park. Being a favourite site for birds to nest that wall is an interesting place; robins, most of the tit family, blackbird, thrush, hedge sparrow, always a redstart with those beautiful deep blue eggs, and never failing, a number of wasp nests. There is a cave of natural formation, long and narrow and always full of dry leaves. Another cave cut into the solid sandstone and with shelves hewn in its walls is man made. It is more or less circular and legend has it that a cobbler plied his trade there. As it is but a short step from the Severn, which it overlooks, one wonders whether it might not have been associated with the barge traffic. Anyway it is still known as Tin Tack's Hole.

Abutting a little circular hill known as Spion Kop there is a magnificent avenue of limes. The choice of site for it was inspired as one comes upon it so unexpectedly. High up on an outermost

Apley Hall – a majestic house in a glorious setting.

branch grows a spray of mistletoe, one of very few growths on the estate. One Christmas Eve two boys brought my heart into my mouth as they were edging out to the coveted prize. I am happy to say both the 'boys' are still going strong! When the limes are in flower there is just one big continuous buzz; a fortnight's harvest for the bees, and that light coloured honey of superb taste.

In the deer-sheds a stunted oak has been favoured for years by nesting kestrels and in a fungus-matted growth in one of the tall Scot's pines there was usually a sparrowhawk's nest. Latterly three small rookeries have been established in the park. Together with several other rookeries on the estate these were only established after a large wood on the west side of the river came under the woodman's axe during World War II.

That wood was known as The Rookery and prior to being felled was the winter roosting place and also nesting site for a huge rook population. On winter evenings they invariably congregated in the tall elms near the Hall, the trees black with them, an unholy medley of sound, but like most of nature's sounds not unpleasing. Possibly they discussed the day's doings, perhaps held a prayer meeting, but whatever it was I am sure it was not idle chatter. Nothing dictatorial about it as they all joined in. After perhaps half an hour's rest they rose with a mighty clatter of wings and voice and crossed the river to settle in The Rookery.

On stormy winter evenings they gave most wonderful displays of aerial gymnastics, looming, diving, twisting in an amazing manner. They are birds of the land and of the air and, most definitely, the treetops. No matter how cold and stormy the night may be they still roost on the topmost branches exposed to everything the weather may send.

There were a few small ponds. One called the Nursery Bank held sizeable tench. Another, the Ice Pool, was fringed with tall reeds which provided roosting quarters for a goodly number of wagtails and the occasional nesting site of reed buntings. At one time ice was collected from it and stored in an ice house in a nearby wood, the Spring Coppice. Later a large pit-hole bedded with bracken in the open was used. Ice was only collected if the temperature was below zero and was immediately covered by a large quantity of bracken. Great pains were taken to ensure against air gaining access and the bracken was piled and trampled down to a depth of several feet. As a means of storing ice the system was remarkably effective and the Hall was kept supplied with ice well into the summer months.

Plover nested on the flat adjoining Morrell's Coppice, also on the elevation of ground near the Hall, the dead bracken in those areas being much to their liking. Alas those liquid notes are no longer heard as none have nested there for several years. In those early days a few pairs nested in practically every sizable field on the estate.

At that time the keepers used to collect their eggs for consumption at the Hall. Searching for the nests was something I always enjoyed doing. There was quite an art in spotting them: it was never to rest the eyes in a particular spot but to keep them sweeping the ground, methodically covering every inch of it whilst keeping a picture of what you were looking for in your mind's eye. That shallow scrape often registered before those wonderfully camouflaged eggs were seen.

This may sound like wholesale destruction but the fact is very few of those early nests ever hatched. Fields had to be harrowed and rolled and, despite the best efforts of the horsemen to save them, clutch after clutch of eggs were destroyed. After a clutch was taken the hen could have laid another and be sitting within a week or ten days. Finally, with the growth of a young crop to shield and shelter them a brood was hatched. Nowadays so few nest in this locality. There is only one explanation I can think of and that is the change in farming methods. In those earlier years plovers were not protected and great numbers were shot, yet those winter flocks were vastly more numerous than is the case today.

Undoubtedly their eggs are a delicacy. Boiled for eight minutes, the whites are not truly white, more shall we say a silvery white. This I stress as it brings to mind the only occasion I ever saw the jelly-like substance ejected by the heron which is so similar in appearance to the white of boiled plover eggs. It is said to be the slimy coating common to all fish which remains undigested and at rare intervals is ejected from the crop. In days gone by it was called 'The Devil's Spawn' by country folk as this mysterious jelly-like substance was an absolute mystery to them.

So far no mention of the deer. When passing through the park I still miss them and often visualise them in their favourite haunts. I still see young fawn leaving the bracken on a summer's evening, one from here and another from there, all joining the

Culling fallow deer in Apley Park. Bill Chaplin (2nd from left),
Norman and brother Ted seated on the bucks,
Edward Sharpe (Snr) with gun over shoulder

bunch and then to the evening's play, stotting straight-legged, and with marvellous leaps. For years the Apley herd was well-managed and boasted many excellent heads. When the second war came along it was done away with and the park land was ploughed up. The Highland cattle had gone many years before to be succeeded by Welsh Black cattle and a flock of Jacob's sheep. Finally the Herefords were given pride of place.

But back to the deer. During the winter they were hand fed when conditions warranted it. Acorns were gathered by children and sometimes their mamas. They received one shilling and three pence (7½p) a bushel and some years as many as three hundred bushels were gathered. Maize, beans and hay were also stored in the deer-sheds for feed. The deer were always fed at the first fall of snow and on being whistled up very quickly appeared despite a lapse of several months since their last feed. Completely without fear! It was a great sight to see them all milling around, proving so very conclusively that animals can think and do remember. Hay was spread out in a ring and if cattle trampled or fouled it the deer refused to touch it no matter how hungry they were.

On still nights during the rutt the clash of horns could be heard at my house a quarter of a mile away and the challenging roar of the bucks was continuous. W. H. Foster was so disturbed one year that a keeper was put on to scare the culprits away from the vicinity of the Hall at night, but with little success.

On one notable occasion an effort to introduce new blood into the herd was not exactly successful. An exchange had been arranged with the Weston Park estate. They arrived complete with deer nets and two young bucks which were turned down. That evening a weary and tired team of men could only claim one solitary capture – and that was one of the young bucks brought from Weston that morning!

Perhaps this is a fitting moment to recall one final little incident involving the deer. Each year the herd had to be culled and very early one morning I was out after the bucks. Only after a very careful stalk had I come within rifle range of several prime beasts slowly moving away from me not far from the Hall. Alarmed, they suddenly halted. Though I could see no reason for their fright it gave me an excellent chance for a shot. Not only had I drawn a bead on one but had actually taken first pressure on the trigger when a form rose from the bracken some eighty yards away and dead in line with my sights. He was pulling up his trousers and it left me with cold shivers running up and down my back! It was old Charlie Wall, out long before his time as it was still not six o'clock in the morning. A valued friend from my earliest days and I had been within a split second of shooting him.

41

THE PATH OF EASE

How often I am told my generation hark back to the past. Perfectly true, and quite right that we should. For who could forget those ragged barefooted boys as I recall them selling newspapers in the streets of Newcastle?

Today our way of living is completely transformed. Yet so many things which matter to me and were so much a part of my own life have been, and still are being lost. Though by no means as arresting and spectacular, some of the greatest changes have occurred in the countryside and I shall be on much safer ground if I stick to that territory. What, for example, has happened to my great love the partridge, fallen alas on evil times these last few years?

It is always difficult to be certain about a wild species so subject to the vagaries of nature but for me their decline began in 1962. During the previous season of 1961, 116 brace were shot on the Bromley beat and on Allscott the following day 84 brace. In 1962, 75 brace were shot in the day at Allscott but the year's total was down to 366 birds, the following two seasons 340 and 201 respectively. From then until the present time 79 is the highest number killed in any season. Over these latter years shooting them has to all intents and purposes been given up. What happened in 1972 was to me something that in my wildest dreams seemed impossible. For the first time in the long records of the Apley game book there was not a single entry in the partridge column.

There is no doubt that adverse weather, scarcity of insects, ants in particular, changes in farming and game management practices, have all contributed to the decline, but these are not in my opinion the main factor. The demise of the partridge is but a minuscule part of the overall scene. Unlike the rest however it is immediately obvious and has been accurately recorded.

In looking at that overall scene let me start by describing the Apley waters of the Severn as they were until the late Forties. At that time the river and valley were delightful. Gravel in the bed of the river was clean and shone. Disturb a stone whilst wading and the loach could be clearly seen for yards as it sought sanctuary elsewhere. Shoals of roach could be seen, their sides flexing and flashing as they stripped algae from the stones.

A succession of water flies hatched throughout the season in countless thousands – so too the midges! There were march browns, mayflies, a wide range of the dun family, the rare yellow sally and a whole host of others. Hawking over the water were swallows, swifts, martins and sandmartins by the score. Wagtails flitted from stone to stone forever tilting up into the air catching their tasty meal. Chaffinches, flycatchers and many others congregated at the riverside snapping up the flying titbits. Trees on the banks were searched by the tit brigade. Hedge sparrows and wrens peered into every nook and cranny of riverbank.

Mallard flighted overhead and in the distance there was the frank (call) of a heron coming into view before alighting in a tall spruce for a quiet look around before dropping down to fish. A fluting sandpiper skimmed the surface with flat flight and settled with dainty dipping tail There was the sleepy hum of bees and insects in the treetops and now and again a shuddering whisper as a slight breeze fanned them then died away. Behind it all the pigeons cooing and soothing of turtledove still more sweet to hear.

The carrion crow's rasping cry and clarion call of a nearby

cock pheasant were common sounds. But before returning to the present let me speak of those pleasant water voles. Coming upon one face to face he would give a startled look and plop he went, swimming just beneath the surface to his underwater hole. On the shingle scattered fish scales lay, the remains of an otter's repast; by the size of the scales it could only have been a chub. A picture of the river as it was then. Well worth recording.

Today there is much the same beauty, some changes along the banks, a few old favourites missing, the big oak at the point of Brown's no longer there, but the pools are more or less as they were when I was young. As the height of the water drops familiar rocks gradually reappear and all seems well.

Alas no! The river is dead. No longer that wealth of fly life hatching out – not even the midges! March brown, grannom or mayfly have not been seen for several years. Those swaying swarms of fly and midge no longer drift in the breeze and the dance of mating duns no longer fills the air. That feast of years gone by is no longer offered, no birdlife, the sky is empty and in the evenings there is neither the large bat high in the sky nor the little fellow skimming the surface with fluttering flight.

No tell-tale work of padded otters or plop of water vole, they too have gone. Even the swans have forsaken the Apley waters. No longer can those flexing roach be seen stripping algae from the river bed. The gravel itself is no longer clean. Move a stone to watch the loach and all you see is a cloud of filthy sediment. Rising shoals of dace or dimpling bleak; they are no longer there. Chaffinch and flycatcher now look elsewhere. A few, so very few wagtails remain. On the river bank vegetation is abnormally strong in growth. Comfrey and charlock to mention but two grow to heights of five and six feet.

Of course by the time it reaches us the Severn has run the gauntlet of human activity for many a long mile. Detergents, untreated sewage, commercial waste, cooling water from power stations, polluted surface water from streets and roads, fluctuations in acidity associated with compensation water, fertiliser run-off – all will have played a part in the transformation described. But there is yet I believe another still more deadly culprit.

It is time to move away from the Severn, but before doing so – just a passing thought. Its rivers are the carriers of the life blood of a country; health can only be associated with purity.

Let us look now at another stretch of water, one which helps feed the Severn; and one which like the Severn I have known intimately since boyhood. Apart from fishing the Long Pool, we derived so much pleasure from the ever-changing panorama of Nature's bountiful richness as the seasons unfolded. Frogs in spring and then later the toads spawned in their hundreds. All around its sides the pool was agitated by the swimming creatures. Literally hundredweights of jelly-like spotted spawn was soon succeeded by countless thousands of tadpoles blackening the water. Later the road right up to our house was alive with baby toads, indeed some even got into the house.

Damselflies adorned the lily leaves, blue ones brilliant in the sun. Water flies hatched in profusion; even mayflies and various duns including the pond olive. There were water fleas and water boatmen and a host of other underwater creatures. Even though the pool was land fed, starwort flourished in it along with other weed. Large dragonflies flashed by, their speed and stopping power remarkable. Swarms of swifts, swallows and martins hawked the water and a host of other small birds joined the feast.

Today the fly life is sadly depleted, frogs have completely disappeared and last year I saw but one toad. Those vivid dragon flies and damsels are non-existent; the small underwater creatures are not there. It is a sad state of affairs.

Now the Long Pool is worthy of special note because it draws its water, every single solitary drop of it from land drainage. A smallish acreage of woodland and a substantial acreage of land which is all under arable rotations. Not a single human dwelling adds any form of pollutant to its catchment area. Unlike the Severn which has flowed so many miles through human habitation we have a pond lying in the very heart of the countryside. Every drop of water in it has drained from the very fields and woodlands of that countryside. No question here of the mayflies, the pond olives, damsels, dragon flies and the host of others having succumbed to urban pollution.

So let us now leave the pool and take the final step back to the land which it drains. Forgetting the partridge for a moment, let me dwell on a few other species with which I am so familiar. First of all my old friend the wasp. Right up until the late Forties and even the mid Fifties I regularly took fifteen to twenty nests within a couple of hundred yards of the house, or perhaps I should say the orchard, for in those days we picked quite a lot of stoned fruit and apples; and I can think of few worse companions on that job! In addition a few more were always taken along the riverside for there again they are bad company should you happen to forget their whereabouts.

This may appear somewhat wholesale destruction of a generally beneficial species but I can assure you that for every nest which was accounted for in this way, brock took scores. Today a thriving nest, tomorrow a newly dug hole with but a few forlorn survivors buzzing hopelessly around the remaining fragments of comb.

Today we have a different picture; but a fraction of their numbers and how often we have remarked on what poorly developed little things they are. Also so many nests apparently established and beginning to thrive suddenly appear to lose vigour and die out. Weather is a dominant factor, always has been, but as with the partridge can in no way fully account for their present state of health.

To return to the frog. Every summer the pit hole was

scythed, laying low its luxuriant crop of nettles and grassy undergrowth. Frogs were to be seen jumping in all directions; all sizes and in a range of colours and shades, olives, browns and greens predominant, each individual frog a thing of beauty.

During the summers of the mid Forties, '46 and '47 if memory serves me correctly, there was a dramatic increase, an explosion in fact, in the grass snake population. This coincided with a great decrease in numbers and we blamed the grass snake for it. After a year or so the snake population returned to normal but the scarcity of frogs remained and has been with us ever since. This change of fortune for the frog was perhaps the most dramatic of all.

Take butterflies. We had them in great numbers and many species; gardens enriched by their beauty and at times decimated by the cabbage variety. Our attics attracted many for their winter hibernation, others came into the outhouses, in fact into the house as well, a favourite place being behind the pictures. Naturally their numbers fluctuated with the warmth of the summers but for every peacock, red admiral, orange tip, brimstone, tortoiseshell, painted lady or cabbage white which visits the garden now there used to be a score.

And what has happened to the ladybirds? And ants too? Where so many patches of scrubland have disappeared and so many steep grassy slopes have finally yielded to the tractor, it is easy to understand but what of the colonies which seemed to thrive everywhere around human habitation?

Before closing this section I should like to dwell on another creature. For as long as I can recall hedgehogs have been part and parcel of the wild scene. Arctic conditions, drought or flood appeared to make little impact on their number. Following the build-up in traffic their abundance was testified by that vast slaughter on the roads. Over the last two years there has been an almost unbelievable fall in numbers.

During the last few months a local keeper has been trying to trap one alive for a friend of his. Having failed to do so he asked neighbouring keepers to get one for him. He is still waiting and hoping. This decline is so much in line with all the others and was certainly not due to road killing.

I have dwelt long enough on this theme to illustrate the point. By no means is the partridge alone in its decline; perhaps indeed in its struggle for survival. Wasps, frogs, toads, butterflies and of course the sparrowhawk has nearly disappeared. You may also add barn owls, grasshoppers, cuckoos, cockchafers, glow worms, moths and dragon flies and even mushrooms. But why go on. These are the sad facts. Where and to what do we look for the solution?

From the observations of a lifetime I am convinced this decline of so many different species is no natural disaster. We need look no further than the modern everyday jargon to which we have all grown so accustomed. It is the language of the 'Ides'; insecticides, herbicides, fungicides, pesticides, molluscicides, aphicides, rodenticides. For practically every weed and pest there is a chemical to destroy. It is along this line a solution will have to be found. Every crop spray is a poison in one way or another and, either directly or indirectly, can in no way be anything but a danger to the partridge and so many other species.

To turn to the brighter side there is growing realisation and genuine concern in many quarters at this state of affairs. Removal of some of the more toxic chemicals, seed dressings in particular, has been undertaken and I feel sure that had this not been achieved I would not have seen my sparrowhawk, the first for many a long month, but yesterday. Although I have no intention of getting involved in discussing them I am also well aware of the social and economic pressures surrounding the use of these products. Least of all, and let me make this quite clear, do I blame farmers for using them; for they like me are men of the countryside and lovers of it. In their position I should have little alternative but to resort, as they do, to the plastic bag and bottle.

What I do say and firmly believe is that our wealth of scientific and technical knowledge, so potentially beneficial to mankind, may yet destroy us all. So many signs laden with fear are pushed aside and the quick path of ease blindly followed.

When I first sat down to write, my sole aim was to share some of the pleasures of a way of life I consider myself so fortunate to have lived. Of course change is continuous, indeed who would wish it otherwise, and any account spanning a lifetime must allow for the fact. For all that I would so dearly have loved to have left a picture, a lasting impression of the countryside as it was up until those years of the late Forties. For I hate to think that future generations may be denied the opportunity to enjoy the beauty and abundance of wildlife which thrived up to that time.

How pleasant to imagine future springtimes alive with cuckoos and anglers as yet unborn gazing in awe at that swaying, sinuous cloud of dancing mayfly shadowing the course of the Worfe. How wonderful to imagine barn owls, those white shadows of mystery and enchantment, quartering landscapes yet to come. Imagine mushroomers again startled by the covey of partridges springing almost beneath their feet and pausing in the dusk to gaze at the wayside glow worm.

As ever, my thoughts drift back to the rivers, that dream of sparkling water and golden trout grown fat on a wealth of insect life, of the ascending salmon and the otter's feast.